VOICES FOR THE VOTE

SHIRE HALL

and the story of Chartism in south Wales

*Modern democracy
starts here*

Zephaniah
Williams

John Frost

Jones
– the
watchmaker

A building in the spotlight...

In this elegant building - Monmouth's Shire Hall - an amazing story, both personal and political, was played out. Three men, who led a Chartist march on Newport, were sentenced to death in one of the most important trials in British legal history.

The plot involves a massed rising of thousands of ordinary people prepared to stand up for their rights; bloodshed and innocent deaths, villains and victims, spies and counter spies, a personal feud, a show trial for sedition, and a young queen about to be married. It is a story which ranges from the Valleys of south Wales to the far flung transportation territory of

Tasmania. It might seem stranger than life, but this is the story of Chartism in Monmouthshire in 1839 and 1840.

You will have to wait for the ending; the climax to this story doesn't come until decades later, when every man and woman in Great Britain secures the right to vote.

Shire Hall,
Agincourt Square,
Monmouth,
1850.

...and a town in the limelight

Politics in Monmouthshire had been controlled for centuries by the great landowning families. In 1839, across Britain, only 1 in 8 men over 21 had the right to vote. Some of the new industrial cities had no political representation at all. The Reform Act of 1832 dashed workers' hopes that they would receive the vote.

Throughout the 1830s Monmouth, the 'County Town', was being sidelined by the industrial growth of Newport and the Monmouthshire Valleys, where ordinary men and women were eager to embrace the ideas of The People's Charter. The Monmouthshire Valleys had the fastest growing population in the UK at this time and no political representation.

For a few weeks during the winter of 1839-40 Monmouth was in the national limelight as its historic courthouse hosted the last mass trial for treason in mainland Britain.

'The Reform Bill does not interfere with the representation of this county, - which returns three members to parliament, namely two for the Shire, and one for the Borough of Monmouth in conjunction with Newport and Usk'.

(Pigot's Directory of 1835)

Monmouth in the early 19th century.

3

What... was Chartism?

The 1830s and 1840s saw Britain in the worst economic recession of the nineteenth century. As living conditions deteriorated working people turned their wrath on a corrupt and privileged Parliament. Chartism became the name for the movement launched by William Lovett when he published the People's Charter in May 1838. So that everyone in Great Britain could have a say in how the country was governed, the Chartists demanded six reforms of Parliament. They organised their campaign around a petition to Parliament, which supporters could sign, demanding the reforms be adopted. Chartists were sent around the country, encouraging men to set up Working Men's Associations and to sign the petition. (There were separate lists for women to sign, over 1000 from Monmouthshire signed.)

To begin with, William Lovett's Charter attracted much interest amongst the middle classes and skilled workmen. As ordinary working people joined in Chartism became a national movement - the first real working class movement in Britain. But Chartists were always divided between those who rejected violent tactics, the 'Moral Force' Chartists, and the 'Physical Force' Chartists, including John Frost from Newport, who argued 'Peacefully if we may, forcibly if we must'.

William Lovett, author of the People's Charter.

What...was the People's Charter?

The six points of the People's Charter were:

- **A vote** for every man over 21.
- **The secret ballot** so you could vote without intimidation.
- **No property qualifications for Members of Parliament (MPs)**, allowing any man, poor or rich to be chosen as an MP.
- **Payment of Members of Parliament**, allowing ordinary working men to be MPs.
- **Equal constituencies** to ensure the same amount of representation for the same number of electors, so that small constituencies didn't swamp the votes of larger ones.
- **Annual Parliaments** - to keep MPs accountable.

We take most of these rights for granted today. But they were hard won rights; men died fighting for them. The struggles of the Chartists shaped democracy in Britain and influenced politics across the world.

John Frost, leader of the Chartists in south Wales.

The cast...

The cast... **for the Chartists:**

Chartists and their establishment enemies

As with any good story there are heroes and villains. Let's introduce some of the men who took leading roles - on both sides.

John Frost
respectable rebel
(1784 - 1877)

Frost was a middle-class draper, who with his wife Mary ran their own shop in Newport's High Street. He announced his support for the People's Charter in October 1838 and soon became the leader of Monmouthshire's Chartists and a speaker for the Chartist cause throughout the country. He had been the Mayor of Newport in 1836 and remained a magistrate until March 1839, when he was removed because of his Chartist activities.

He was described by the editor of the *Monmouthshire Merlin* as, *'about five feet seven inches in height, rather stoutly formed; his personal appearance and manner are rather at variance with recklessness or violence of conduct or character. The expression of his countenance is mild and thoughtful; and his manner would be regarded as indicating more than usual benevolence and kindness of disposition. In the tones of his voice, too both in conversation and when speaking in public, there is something pleasing and conciliatory'.*

Henry Vincent
the performer
(1813 - 1873)

Twenty-five year old Henry Vincent was by far the most entertaining of the Chartists. An eloquent speaker, with a fine singing voice and a talent for mimicry, he joined the London Working Men's Association in 1837 and was one of the original signatories to the Charter. He was sent to Wales by the London Chartists as a 'paid missionary', to spread support for the People's Charter and during the spring of 1839 he addressed mass meetings across Monmouthshire.

Vincent was also the publisher of a Chartist newspaper, *The Western Vindicator* and he wrote a witty weekly account of his travels called *Life and Rambles*: *'Left Bristol at two o'clock in the steam-packet for Newport, in South Wales.*

Had a very rough passage. I observed two Newport Whigs reaching dreadfully. I think I must have agitated their internals, and they were trying to throw me off.'

Zephaniah Williams
the blunt, bold talker
(1795 - 1874)

Welsh-speaking Williams became the spokesperson for the Chartists in the western valleys of Monmouthshire. He had been employed as a mineral agent for the Sirhowy Company, an influential and powerful position, but left in early 1839 to run the Royal Oak Inn with his wife Joan, in Blaina, just as the Chartist movement took off in Monmouthshire. He held strong radical views, favouring a republic and doubting Christian belief. He had been in trouble with the authorities, who described him as *'5ft 8 inches, of strong, square build, a bold talker with a blunt manner and a swaggering walk'.*

Dr. William Price
colourful republican
(1800-1893)

Price was one of the more colourful Chartists, a republican with an interest in pagan Druidism. He was a doctor employed to look after the workers at the cable works in Pontypridd, where he founded a Chartist lodge. A popular Welsh speaker amongst the colliers of the coalfield, he was very influential with the Aberdare and Merthyr Chartist lodges. He had a strong following and there were many who saw him, rather than John Frost, as the leader of the Chartists in south Wales.

William Jones
militant actor
(1809 - 1873)

Jones was the energetic and militant leader of the Chartists in the more anglicised Eastern Valley, north of Pontypool, where he had moved from Bristol in 1833. He worked as a watchmaker and, with his wife, kept the Bristol House beer shop where he established the Pontypool Working Men's Association. Although of Welsh extraction he didn't speak Welsh. He had been a travelling actor and proved to be a popular performer at Chartist gatherings throughout the Monmouthshire coalfield.

Supporting Cast:

John Rees

(alias 'Jack the Fifer') a mysterious figure who boasted military experience, having served in the New Orleans Greys during the Texan War of Independence in 1835 - 36. He was described by the authorities as *'a mason working at the Tredegar ironworks'*.

William Lovett

(1800 - 1877) He was the Secretary of the London Working Men's Association and the author of the People's Charter. A cabinet maker by trade, he was a vocal campaigner for political rights for workers. Brought up by his widowed mother in the Cornish fishing village of Newlyn, he learnt to read and write at the local Methodist church.

Feargus O'Connor

(1794 - 1855) was the publisher of the *Northern Star* Chartist newspaper, and a prominent national figure in the Chartist movement. He raised money to pay for Frost's defence and was in Monmouth throughout his trial. He was the only Chartist to gain election to Parliament in Nottingham in 1847. Over 50,000 people attended his funeral in 1855.

Thomas Prothero
Vengeful villain
(1780 - 1853)

Prothero had been engaged in a longstanding feud with John Frost, dating back to the 1820s. Frost had published pamphlets accusing Prothero of corruption whilst he was Newport Town Clerk. Prothero's revenge was a libel case. Frost was found guilty and served six months in gaol. Prothero took any opportunity to pursue his long time enemy.

Thomas Phillips
Prothero's protégé
(1801 - 1867)

Legal partner and political ally of Prothero, together they prevented Frost from being re-elected Mayor of Newport in 1837, and used their influence to have Frost sacked as a magistrate when he became involved with Chartism. Phillips was elected Mayor of Newport in 1838. He was a Welsh speaker and in the late 1840s he became a leading defender of the language and culture of Wales.

Lieutenant Gray
of the 45th Foot Regiment
(1810 - 1889)

Born in Ceylon, into a military family, Basil Gray was a young Lieutenant in the 45th Foot Regiment which was garrisoned at the Workhouse in Newport in November 1839. The Regiment had recently returned from a long tour of duty in the Far East, India and Ceylon. He was promoted to Captain following the Rising, but lived on half pay in London for much of his later life.

Capel Hanbury Leigh
(1776 - 1861) the Lord Lieutenant of Monmouthshire, lived at Pontypool House, where he kept London informed of Chartist activities in the county. With few police and no armed forces, he called for the power to swear in special constables, arm the gentry and suppress sedition.

Reginald Blewitt MP
(1799 - 1878) elected for the Monmouthshire Boroughs (Monmouth, Usk and Newport) in 1837, had a firm finger on the pulse of local politics and business. He owned the *Monmouthshire Merlin* newspaper, collieries in Cwmbran and a Newport bank, served as Deputy Lord Lieutenant and lived at Llantarnam Abbey, which he renovated extravagantly at a cost of £60,000.

The first Working Men's Association in Wales was set up in Carmarthen in 1837, by solicitor Hugh Williams, a close friend of William Lovett. Soon the National Petition was circulating in Welsh, striking a chord with workers from the coalfield who were attracted to this new movement which offered hope for a better future.

In one of the most highly industrialised areas in Britain at the time, the Monmouthshire Valleys, Chartism flourished. John Frost announced his support for the People's Charter in 1838 and soon became the leader of Monmouthshire's Chartists, as Working Men's Associations were set up in Pontypool and Newport. He launched the Charter in Newport at the Parrot Inn, where he addressed a crowd of over 300 from an upstairs window. When Henry Vincent arrived in Wales in January 1839 he mesmerised Welsh audiences with his clever impersonations and fiery speeches. Soon there were more than thirty Chartist groups or Working Men's 'lodges' in Monmouthshire alone.

Although Chartism in Wales was hugely influenced by the English movement, (and recorded from an English perspective through the press) there was a distinctly Welsh dimension. Many Welsh people had been influenced by the ideas of Tom Paine, whose 'Rights of Man' had been published in Welsh. Many more, including Zephaniah Williams and Dr Price had grown up with an inherited Welsh tradition of *the cause of justice* and *a rising* against the invaders. The Carmarthen solicitor Hugh Williams even created a Chartist flag which referred back to Welsh bardic traditions: green represented the earth, blue the heavens and white represented *Justice* or *Cyfiawnder*.

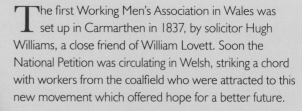

John Frost

Newport, Caerleon and Pontypool Working Men's Associations elected John Frost as their delegate to the National Convention, which gathered in London during February 1839.

We, the poor remnants of Ancient Britons, are confined to the mountains of Wales, cultivating an ungrateful soil, whose production is insufficient to support its occupiers. The tendancy of our boasted constitution to accumulate property into few hands, and the present wretched mode of taxing the produce of labour and the necessities of life, has of late increased the number of our poor into an alarming degree, and must sooner or later reduce the labouring classes into a servile dependency or absolute slavery, and which the insatiable avarice of the landed gentry has partly effected in our country.

Chartists found a receptive audience in Wales, many of whom were familiar with the sentiments of Welsh Republican, William Jones, from Llancadfan.

Liquid inspiration

Most Chartist 'lodges' met in public houses, electing officers and collecting regular subscriptions. Two of the Chartist leaders were landlords. Zephaniah Williams ran the Royal Oak in Blaina and William Jones ran the Bristol House beer shop in Pontypool, although some leading Chartists, including Henry Vincent, were total abstainers.

As pubs became important Chartist meeting places many landlords found their premises were the front line in the battle with the authorities. In April 1839 the Mayor of Newport, Thomas Phillips, nicknamed 'Mr Gag', banned meetings in the town's pubs. This drove the Chartists into secret gatherings in industrial outbuildings in Pillgwenlly and in the beer houses of slum land along Newport's river bank - Friar's Field (where many Newport Chartists would seek refuge following the attack on the Westgate).

Magistrates also tried to control the growth of Chartism by banning landlords from serving Chartists. In Monmouth the licensee of the Masons Arms in Monnow Street was summoned to appear before the Mayor to explain why he allowed men who called themselves 'Chartists' to drink in his pub. He was told to refuse to serve them in future, or face a penalty.

James Horner held regular readings of Chartist newspapers at the Prince of Wales pub in Newport.

Female Patriots

The Chartist movement welcomed women. They attended mass meetings, marched in rallies and even named their children after their Chartist heroes! They were some of Vincent's most enthusiastic supporters and when he arrived at Pontllanfraith in March 1839 a hundred girls with flags and flowers led him from the Greyhound to the Coach and Horses in Blackwood. Vincent wanted votes for women as well as for all men.

The Newport Female Patriotic Society organized tea parties and recitals in support of the Charter. On one occasion, a local butcher's daughter, Miss Dickenson, who played the piano, joined Henry Vincent in leading 300 women out in to Newport High Street for an impromptu procession and public meeting. As Vincent wrote in *Rambles*, *'I explained the principles of the Charter... and appealed to the ladies for assistance, encouragement, and support .....The Newport ladies are progressing with great spirit to the terror of the Aristocrats of the town and neighbourhood'.*

Mary Brewer came to the forefront as a Chartist organiser in Newport, following the imprisonment of Henry Vincent and her brother, William Edwards. She collected lodge subscriptions and sold Chartist newspapers. Elsewhere landladies of public houses also roused support. Joan Williams, the wife of Zephaniah Williams, organised the Blaina Female Chartist lodge that met at their beer house, the Royal Oak. There were similar associations in Blackwood, Pontllanfraith, Pontypool, Abersychan and Merthyr Tydfil.

Over a thousand Monmouthshire women signed the National Petition to Parliament in 1839. Counted separately, women contributed one in five of all signatures, even though the Charter would not give them the vote. With women involved, Chartism in south Wales developed as a family movement and many of the mass Chartist meetings of the summer of 1839 were family affairs with a carnival atmosphere. Some in authority put the blame for Chartist activities firmly on women, who had urged their men folk on.

The great meeting of the Birmingham Political Union in 1832 - forerunner of the massed Chartist gatherings of 1839.

Looking for new and peaceful ways to show their frustration with the electoral system, Chartists began a series of church 'sit-ins'. In April 1839 Henry Vincent sat in silence with his supporters in the congregation at St. Paul's Church in Newport. The anti-Chartist sermon delivered by Rev. James Francis was intended as a warning. He knew there were a number of sympathisers in his congregation, including two well-known Chartists - John Lovell and Charles Waters - who sang in the choir.

With his silent 'sit in' Henry Vincent was making a very serious statement against the Church of England which was siding with the state and not allowing people to represent their grievances and demands. Vincent understood the nature of the propaganda war that the Church had joined as pulpits were increasingly being used for anti-Chartist purposes, stressing the stupidity of Chartist activity and denouncing Chartists as criminals and atheists.

There is no convincing evidence to show that Rev. Francis persuaded any of his working class visitors to abandon Chartism. It's also very unlikely that any of them would have been amongst the 500 subscribers for the printed version of the sermon offered for sale in the *Monmouthshire Merlin* newspaper. His sermon went down well with most of his regular congregation and it became the 'talk of the town'. Fear of revolution was gripping the local gentry and upper business class. The French Revolution of 1789-99 still loomed large in their imaginations.

The Church sit-in at St Pauls was probably the first in the country, signalling a new peaceful protest tactic. During the summer of 1839 'sit-ins' followed at St. Woolos, at Hope Chapel in Skinner Street, Newport, and in Pontypool and Merthyr.

Many Nonconformist congregations were sympathe Chartism, but few ministers and elders were willing meetings on chapel premises, fearing plans and plots hatched. It was not unusual for Chartists to ask a pre give a sermon to show the theological arguments fo force Chartism. An Independent Minister in Aberdar reassurance that there were no physical force Char the congregation before he preached on the rights and the oppression inherent in Toryism!

Although Chartism grew from Nonconformist roots, show that some Chartists were excommunicated fr chapels. William Wise was excluded from Trosnant Church in Pontypool, for being implicated in Chartist The Rev. Thomas Thomas, delivered a sermon in N 1839 that distanced the Baptist cause from 'physical This was published in London as 'The civil duties of C as occasioned by the late outrages at Newport'. He

Part of the propaganda war, waged through the press and the church, included printing political (rather than theological) sermons.

This Day is Published, pr
THE CIVIL DUTIES OF CI
occasioned by the LATE OUTRA
outhshire, preached at the English
By THOMAS TH
Published by Wightman, 24, Pater
old by Prosser and Evans, Pontypoo
enkins, Cardiff; Heath, Monmouth
ley, Abergavenny.

St. Woolos

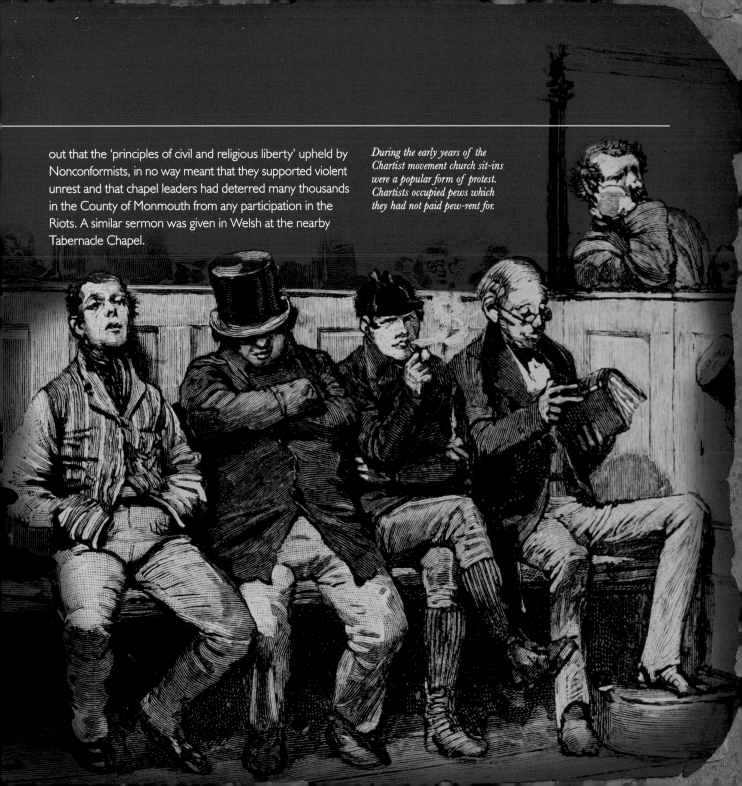

out that the 'principles of civil and religious liberty' upheld by Nonconformists, in no way meant that they supported violent unrest and that chapel leaders had deterred many thousands in the County of Monmouth from any participation in the Riots. A similar sermon was given in Welsh at the nearby Tabernacle Chapel.

During the early years of the Chartist movement church sit-ins were a popular form of protest. Chartists occupied pews which they had not paid pew-rent for.

A hero imprisoned

Throughout the spring of 1839 Henry Vincent rallied support for the Charter in communities across Monmouthshire. Concerned with his enthusiastic reception Thomas Phillips, the Mayor of Newport, began to attend Chartist meetings to gather evidence which might help silence Vincent. In April, Phillips was especially alarmed to hear Henry Vincent speak in Newport. Although Vincent urged people to keep the peace his language was strong *'...perish the privileged orders! death to the aristocracy!'*

Capel Hanbury Leigh, the Lord Lieutenant of Monmouthshire, lost no time in writing to the Home Secretary, reminding him that there were no soldiers or special constables for miles around. Across south Wales there were only twenty paid policemen and the nearest soldiers were stationed in Brecon. Vincent mocked the authorities in his diary: *'The foolish magistrates had issued a proclamation, forbidding our meeting, and calling all Chartist meetings illegal....... Rumour was abroad that I should be arrested in the evening. At seven o'clock several thousand people assembled, joined me at Mr Frost's, and conducted me in procession through the town...... there could not have been less than 8,000 persons present. The Mayor and several magistrates were there. I spoke for two hours and a half, in a very animated strain.'*

Keep the peace poster.

TO THE
Men & Women
OF
NEWPORT.

MY FRIENDS,

You have ever found me your consistent and dauntless advocate, I have a right, therefore, to expect you are my Friends.

I am informed upon unquestionable authority that your local rulers are anxious to arrest me to night. LET THEM TAKE ME. If their conduct be legal---*well!* If illegal, they shall hereafter rue it. At the worst my detention can but be for a few days---and as Philosophy is every thing, the jails of our tyrants do not appal me.

Efforts are being made to frighten the people by calling our meetings illegal.---I never attended an illegal meeting---and there have been none of an illegal nature held within the precints of Newport, *save one held lately at Christchurch, where a man named Phillips told the mob to make their horses stand fire, and keep their powder dry!*

I am told your Magistrates are about to swear in persons as Special Constables. They have their reasons for so doing; I believe them to be bad ones, and will with your assistance, turn the mischief they may contemplate into an engine for their own legal destruction.

Meet me to night at Pentonville, where I shall do myself the honour of addressing you.

Keep the Peace I charge you!---The slightest indications of tumult on our part would afford our enemies a pretext for letting loose their Bloodhounds on us.

Keep the Peace
and laugh your enemies to scorn!
Your devoted Friend,
HENRY VINCENT.

APRIL 25th, 1839.

John Partridge, Printer, Newport

The King's Head Hotel in Newport, where Henry Vincent was taken following his arrest in May 1839.

Vincent remained free but it was only a matter of time before his arrest in London on May 7th 1839. Three days later he appeared before the Magistrates in Newport. His diary records what happened: *'Arrived in Newport at three o'clock. The people loudly cheered me. Several fights took place in the streets between the people and the specials, AND THE SPECIALS WOULD HAVE BEEN CUT UP LIKE MINCED MEAT IF THE CHARTIST LEADERS HAD NOT ORDERED THE PEOPLE TO KEEP THE PEACE. I listened to the depositions; suffice to say THEY ARE ALL FULL OF LIES, MISTATEMENTS, AND FLAWS! The fool Phillips (the fellow who is Mayor, or more properly speaking ass), said, we be bound over to appear at the assizes – myself in ONE THOUSAND POUNDS.'*

Fearing an uprising, the magistrates imposed bail terms and moved Vincent to the County Gaol at Monmouth where he was held for nearly seven weeks before a judge ordered his release. His trial on 2nd August 1839, at the Shire Hall, aroused much interest in the town. The court was filled with 'elegantly dressed ladies' and their 'gentlemen friends' who reportedly hissed the counsel for Vincent's defence. Outside, large crowds shouted 'Vincent for ever' when he left the court for the gaol, having been found guilty of attending illegal meetings and sentenced to a year's imprisonment.

Three other Chartists from Newport, men who helped organise the meetings Vincent spoke at, were sentenced to prison terms of six to nine months. All upright respectable businessmen - William Edwards a baker and brother of Mary Brewer, John Dickenson a butcher and father of Miss Dickenson and William Townshend Jnr, son of a merchant

and victualler - their punishment caused much distress in the town and explains why Frost expected a good reception for his marchers later in the year.

Chartists were enraged by Vincent's imprisonment. The debate, between those Chartists who believed in using moral argument to secure the Charter points, and those who believed physical force would be the only way to secure change, intensified.

Petition and protest

By June 1839 one and a quarter million people had signed a petition calling for the People's Charter to be adopted. The petition, nearly three miles in length, was presented to Parliament, who immediately rejected it. Playing straight into the hands of the physical force Chartists, the public mood now turned aggressive. The Charter had become the symbol of protest for all who felt excluded from political power and were angry about unfair taxes, aristocratic privilege and the brutal workhouse poor law. Poor relations between employers and employees added to the growing atmosphere of hostility and suspicion. What could the Chartists do when Parliament refused to change the election system?

The *Western Vindicator*, Vincent's Chartist newspaper, continued to be published despite his imprisonment, and reported in August 1839:

'There is something more in hand with the people at the present time than a mere question of a rise or fall in wages. They feel the degradation of being bound by laws, oppressive and tyrannical...made by persons who know nothing of their condition and their wants. They have felt there is ...no hope of any amelioration from a parliament elected by you... the middle classes. They have been slaves,... and they are determined to be so not much longer.'

PREAMBLE

We, your petitioners, dwell in a land whose merchants are noted for enterprise, whose manufacturers are very skilful, and whose workmen are proverbial for their industry.

The land itself is goodly, the soil rich, and the temperature wholesome; it is abundantly furnished with the materials of commerce and trade; it has numerous and convenient harbours; in facility of internal communication it exceeds all others.

Yet, with all these elements of national prosperity, and with every disposition and capacity to take advantage of them, we find ourselves overwhelmed with public and private suffering.

We are bowed down under a load of taxes; which, notwithstanding, fall greatly short of the wants of our rulers; our traders are trembling on the verge of bankruptcy; our workmen are starving; capital brings no profit, and labour no remuneration; the home of the artificer is desolate, and the warehouse of the pawnbroker is full; the workhouse is crowded, and the manufactory is deserted.

The energies of a mighty kingdom have been wasted in building up the power of selfish and ignorant men, and its resources squandered for their aggrandisement.

Required, as we are universally, to support and obey the laws, nature and reason entitle us to demand that in the making of the laws, the universal voice shall be implicitly listened to. We perform the duties of freemen; we must have the privileges of freemen. Therefore, we demand universal suffrage. The suffrage, to be exempt from the corruption of the wealthy and the violence of the powerful, must be secret.

Preamble to the National Charter petition.

Twenty thousand people in south Wales were paid up members of the Chartist movement. They believed that the right to vote would change their lives. At the end of October Frost wrote to the farmers and tradesmen of Monmouthshire, stating that unless the Charter became law quickly, there would be no security for property or people. Strangely the authorities appeared to believe the threat from Chartism had gone. On 2nd November the *Monmouthshire Merlin* included a headline, *'Extinction of Chartism'*.

THE MONMOUTHSHIRE MERLIN.

CIRCULATING THROUGH THE COUNTIES OF

MONMOUTH, BRECON, AND THE WHOLE OF SOUTH WALES, GLOUCESTERSHIRE, HEREFORDSHIRE, BRISTOL, &c.

"THE MAGIC OF THE MIND."—BYRON

A language of sedition...

...and a language of suppression

'I regret my ignorance of the Welch. It appears to be a powerfully impressive language, and the people are passionately fond of their mother tongue.'

(Henry Vincent, *Rambles*)

The secrecy of the Chartists' plans were assisted in no small part by the fact that so many Chartists spoke a language few in authority understood - Welsh. In 1839 Monmouthshire was still a Welsh-speaking county, although it was in a state of flux. During the first half of the 19th century the majority of incomers to western Monmouthshire spoke Welsh. It was the language of the working classes, especially of the colliers of the Black Domain. English was more widespread amongst workers in the iron industries and along the eastern border and in Newport where English was the first language. Migration in and out of the county reflected the constant search for work.

The two Monmouthshire Chartists leaders, John Frost and Zephaniah Williams both spoke Welsh, and although Frost didn't speak in public in Welsh, he would have used it daily in his business. When Frost had been in gaol in 1822 his *'chief concern was to obtain a good knowledge of Welsh and French'*, so that he would be a more formidable opponent of Thomas Phillips. At lodge meetings it was often Zephaniah Williams' role to explain in Welsh, whilst William Jones, who had no Welsh, spoke in English. Dr William Price was also a passionate Welsh-speaker.

English predominated among the landowning capitalists and professional classes who had moved into the area from England much earlier. For them English was the language of law and order. With the exception of men such as Newport Mayor Thomas Phillips, few people were bilingual in the sense we use the term today. Most were monolingual, only speaking Welsh, English, or even Irish.

Mutual suspicion and fear flourished where many people understood little of their neighbours' language. The establishment - clergymen of the Church of England, magistrates and landowners - all agreed that Welsh was a secret language used by Chartists. The press reported, after the Rising, that it was easier for the Chartists to plan in secret, *'where the lower orders speak a language unknown to the educated classes'* (*Morning Chronicle*, 7th November 1839). This paranoia was nothing new. During the French Revolution some Welsh-speaking societies in London had been raided on the grounds that their members could be spies and revolutionaries.

Welsh helped keep Chartist plans secret, whilst the remote geography of the Monmouthshire hills was a significant advantage as Vincent noted, *'I could not help thinking of the defensible nature of the country in the case of foreign invasion! A few thousands of armed men on the hills could successfully defend them. Wales would make an excellent Republic.'*

Quietly, in another language, and out of sight, the Chartists started organising. As summer turned to autumn the political movement became a front for a military organisation - drilling, arming, training. Secret cells were set up, covert meetings were held in the Chartist Caves at Llangynidyr and weapons were manufactured. Behind closed doors and in pub back rooms plans were drawn up for a mass Chartist protest.

Soldiers and spies

Both sides were making plans. The authorities were anxious that Chartism was recruiting supporters from many sections of society. Expecting trouble they stationed troops in towns and cities across Britain, and in response to a request for soldiers, a contingent of the 29th Lancers arrived in Newport at the beginning of May 1839.

Traditionally troops were billeted in inns and houses, as this was cheap, but there was concern that soldiers were being influenced by Chartist ideas. There had been attempts by local Chartist leaders to persuade men to desert. Although most stayed loyal to their officers, rising desertion rates helped feed Chartist hopes that the troops would not fire on them.

The 45th Foot Regiment replaced the Lancers in Newport in September. Not long returned from a tour of duty in India, the authorities felt that they would be more reliable. They were billeted in the new Workhouse at Stow, to prevent fraternisation with local people.

The government also established a network of informers and spies to infiltrate Chartist meetings. Frost knew of rumours of spies among the hills, men whose role was to incite the Chartists to acts of violence. One man who called himself David Jones and was probably from London had been at Vincent's first Chartist meeting in Wales on January 1st 1839. He had taken copious notes of Vincent's speech:

'Mr Vincent said ...the House of Commons was a long room ….. with a lot of fellows sitting round some drunk & some asleep,.... He said the House of Commons were fools & enemies of the Working Man, & that some fine morning the people would rise ….. & would not the men of Wales assist the men of England in compelling them to pass the Charter.'

David Jones was undoubtedly a spy. During the weekend of the Rising he was seen throughout the Eastern Valley, but he managed to evade capture and imprisonment.

Uniforms of the 45th Foot Regiment.

The march

Final plans for the mass protest were made at the Coach and Horses in Blackwood where, on Friday 1st November, men from thirty Chartist lodges met. Three massed groups of Chartists were to march to Newport, one from the Rhymney and Sirhowy valleys led by John Frost, another down the Ebbw valleys led by Zephaniah Williams. And a third from the Eastern Valley directed by William Jones. Williams said they were going to Newport to show they were determined to get the Charter made the law of the land. He reassured Chartists no one would be hurt and that the soldiers garrisoned at the Workhouse would not touch them. They were to carry weapons in self-defence and march in units of ten men.

And it was at the Coach and Horses on Sunday 3rd November that John Frost was seen wearing a great coat and a red cravat around his neck, pacing up and down as if awaiting a signal. Throughout the night Chartists gathered at meeting points, until thousands were on the road, marching towards Newport in torrential rain. The weather was foul, seriously hampering their progress, and there was no sign of William Jones and his contingent at the planned meeting point outside Newport. Many people were out and about under cover of darkness; some Chartists were captured and taken to the Westgate Hotel.

Early on Monday morning the bedraggled and exhausted miners and iron workers from the Monmouthshire Valleys met up with Newport Chartists, who guided them into town, to avoid the soldiers stationed at the Workhouse.

Eagerly acting as John Frost's lieutenant on the march, Jack the Fifer (John Rees of Tredegar) headed the column of four thousand Chartists as they marched down Stow Hill. An army deserter called Williams and Dai the Tinker (another man called David Jones) were at the front, as well as John Frost and other Newport Chartists - Wright Beatty, Charles Waters and John Lovell. Zephaniah Williams was at the back, urging stragglers on, ensuring nobody targeted the Workhouse or magistrates' houses in the town.

Armed with their picks, pikes and guns and marching in orderly ranks, the men turned the corner at the bottom of Stow Hill and lined up outside the Westgate Hotel, shouting 'Give us up the Prisoners' (although the Prosecution maintained they said 'Give yourselves up as our prisoners').

'...At about nine o'clock the cheering of many voices was heard in the distance, from the direction of Stowhill, producing the utmost alarm, as evidenced by the countenances of those inhabitants who appeared at their windows. In a few minutes after, the front ranks of a numerous body of men approached, armed with weapons of every description – guns, pistols, blunderbusses, swords, bayonets, daggers, pikes.......bill-hooks, reaping-hooks, hatchets, cleavers, axes, pitchforks, blades of knives, scythes and saws fixed in staves, pieces of iron.... in fact every kind of weapon that could be at all made available.'

Contemporary map showing in red the route the marchers took down Stow Hill to the Westgate Hotel.

Dreadful riot and loss of life at Newport

At the request of Mayor Phillips, the 45th Regiment had divided its force between the Workhouse and the Westgate Hotel, where the Mayor and the magistrates hoped to control the unrest. Inside the hotel were thirty soldiers from the 45th who had moved into position only minutes before the Chartists arrived. Hidden behind shuttered windows and unseen from the street, they were only feet away from the front line of a volatile crowd. Most of the soldiers were drawn from the working classes; they didn't have the right to vote either.

Finding that the gates on the side of the Westgate were locked, the Chartists moved towards the front door which was manned by the special constables. Did they know that, inside, the soldiers under the command of Lieutenant Gray were poised for battle?

A gun fired, windows were smashed and some Chartists pushed into the hallway of the Hotel. According to the *Monmouthshire Merlin* the soldiers '*fired over the shutters which were nearly mid-way up the window*

but it was supposed that the balls passed over the heads of the visitors'. The report goes on to say that the shutters were opened and, clutching a copy of the Riot Act that had been printed and issued early that morning, Mayor Phillips appeared at the window as if about to address the rebels when he received a slug through the left arm. The 28 soldiers led by Sergeants Daily and Armstrong filed past the windows, firing their muskets in quick succession at the crowd. This surprise tactic forced mass retreat.

Many fell to the ground dead, including an army deserter known as Williams, who was shot dead by Lieutenant Gray. Jack the Fifer, despite a hand injury, urged a fight back and a small band of determined fighters returned fire, including by some accounts, a one legged man with a wooden leg who stood and fired three rounds in reply! Some of the soldiers turned their guns on those who had entered the hotel.

The Chartist Riots at Newport.

Just Published, by R. TAYLOR, Price One Shilling,

A LITHOGRAPHIC DRAWING, Twelve inches by Nine, by an eminent Artist, representing the attack on the Westgate Hotel, Newport, at the time the assailants fired upon the soldiers.
To be had of Mr. Farror and Mrs. Heath, Monmouth; Mr. R. Taylor, Chepstow; Messrs. Webber and Son, Newport; the Booksellers at Cardiff; and Mrs. Bingham, Broad-street, Bristol; and Farror and Dobles, Ross.

*Advertisement from the
Monmouthshire Merlin
January 18th 1840.*

Artists 'cashed in' on the public appetite for blood and action. Howell pictured an ambushed Westgate Hotel with guns firing from several windows. Taylor's prints, based on his official drawings (see page 40), held to the army's line that they fired only from the bay windowed room to the left of the crowd.

As soon as the battle commenced, John Frost fled in dismay, three unused pistols in his coat pocket. *'The moment I saw blood flow I became terrified and fled'*, Frost admitted. Fighting lasted about twenty minutes, before the last Chartist left the scene or fell, but the military remained in position for at least another hour. The authorities were not convinced of their hold on the town, aware that many Chartists from the Eastern Valley, led by William Jones, had gathered near Newport Castle. On hearing news of the carnage, this 'reserve army' stayed away. A stunned Zephaniah Williams wandered off, crying when he realised that Chartists had lost their lives.

The Dead

'While we write, the wounds of many of the deluded persons engaged in that affair are still fresh and bleeding and the lifeless bodies of others remain grim and melancholy spectacles of the lamentable event'.
(Reported in the *Monmouthshire Beacon*, November 9th 1839)

The following have been identified as amongst the dead:

John Codd

David Davies of Waunhelygen, Brynmawr

- Davies, son of the above

Evan Davies, collier

John Davis of Pontnewynydd, carpenter

William Evans of Tredegar, miner

William Farraday of Blackwood, collier

John Jonathan of Blaina (probably)

William Griffiths of Merthyr

Robert Lansdown

Reece Meredith of Tredegar

David Morgan of Tredegar, tinker

John Morris, miner

George Shell of Pontypool, carpenter

Abraham Thomas of Blaina, collier

Isaac Thomas of Nantyglo

-Williams, a deserter from the 29th Regiment of Foot

William Williams of Cwmtillery

'William Aberdare'

'John the Roller' of Nantyglo

The tally was at least twenty dead and more than sixty wounded. The Welsh language paper *Seren Gomer* reported that after the rioters dispersed, a young girl pushed her way through the throng of spectators at the Westgate, and as soon as she caught sight of the bloodied bodies, fell on one of them, giving a heartbreaking scream, embracing and kissing it; when she was taken away, her arms and face were covered in his blood. This rioter, who had come to such a pitiful end, was her sweetheart!

The *Monmouthshire Merlin* wrote that, 'A few of the miserable objects that were helplessly and mortally wounded continued to writhe in tortures, crying for water'. And for over an hour a young apprentice carpenter lay wounded near the steps of the Westgate Hotel before Moses Scard, a special constable, was allowed by the soldiers to give him some water, just before he died. George Shell's body was amongst the ten buried by the military in two unmarked graves at St. Woolos under cover of darkness. Their names were not entered in the church's burial register and only Shell's name appears in the local registry records. The *Monmouthshire Beacon* published a letter that Shell had written to his parents before joining the march, although some questioned its authenticity:

Dear Parents,
I hope this will find you as well, as I am myself at present. I shall this night be engaged in a struggle for freedom and should it please God to spare my life, I shall see you soon; but if not, grieve not for me, I shall fall in a noble cause. My tools are at Mr. Cecil's, and likewise my clothes.

Yours truly, George Shell.

Frightful wounds

Many of the wounded died later and were buried secretly. Edward Dowling, editor of the *Merlin* wrote, *Many who suffered in the fight crawled away; some exhibiting frightful wounds….Others, desperately maimed, were carried in the arms of the humane for medical aid'*. The ironmaster Samuel Homfray reckoned there were thirty casualties; the authorities were keen to play down the numbers.

Faced with widespread rumours of death amongst the 45th, Lieutenant Gray insisted that their only casualty was Sergeant James Daily, who was seen to collapse with six slugs in his head. They refused to admit there were others. Yet, army records reveal that at least one other soldier, Sergeant John Armstrong, was injured. Both sergeants were retired from active service and offered posts and accommodation at the Tower of London. Daily mysteriously never took up his appointment as a Yeoman of the Queen's Guard. Armstrong served as a Yeoman Warder and when he died three years later, aged 38, he was buried at the Tower.

Amongst the civilian forces, Mayor Phillips suffered most with wounds in his left arm and right groin who, 'faint from loss of blood, was carried upstairs' in the Westgate. Some of the special constables were injured: Henry Williams (ironmonger) was stabbed, Edward Morgan (draper) received a gunshot wound 'the ball was extracted and he has since completely recovered') and John O'Dwyer and several others were trampled underfoot at the front entrance to the Westgate. Thomas Walker suffered a six inch stab wound in his thigh during a confrontation with a group of Chartists near the Welsh Oak at Cefn, whilst out scouting on horseback during the night.

30 Irish soldiers save the British Empire from revolution!

The Chartist march on Newport was the peak of popular armed resistance in the fight for the right to vote in Britain. Thirty soldiers, two thirds of whom were Irish, stayed loyal and maintained order for a country which did not allow them to vote. The soldiers believed they had acted within the law when they opened fire; a magistrate was present and they were fired upon first. An Irish politician, Daniel O' Connell, delighted in telling Parliament that 30 Irish soldiers had saved the British Empire from revolution! The Chartist's *Western Vindicator* had another view:

Moral force has failed. And alas! Physical force has failed like wise. We cannot fight against armed bodies of well organised butchers of mankind.

Daniel O'Connell

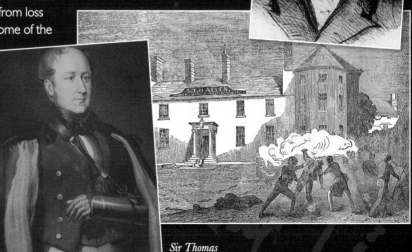

Sir Thomas Phillips

£100 reward *for wanted men*

Immediately rewards of £100 were offered for John Frost, Zephaniah Williams, William Jones, Jack the Fifer (John Rees), and David the Tinker. Frost was captured that night, eating bread and cheese at the house in Newport of his friend, the printer John Partridge. William Jones evaded capture for a week, and was found in woods near Crumlin, whilst Zephaniah Williams was found three weeks later on board a ship in Cardiff about to leave for Portugal. The authorities failed to find Jack the Fifer who escaped to America, or his accomplice, David the Tinker.

Almost a year later, the offer of a reward winkled out Wright Beatty, who had led some of the western valleys men through

Rogerstone to Newport. Dr William Price who had helped to plan the Rising, didn't trust Frost's leadership, and had refused to march the men of Pontypridd to Newport. Believing he was a wanted man, as he had been stirring up Chartists around Pontypridd, Price escaped to Paris disguised in women's clothes. William David, another leader from the Pontypridd area, reached the USA. Both returned within a few years; neither was charged.

Interrogation

Frost's old enemy Thomas Prothero took on the role of chief interrogator. He was delighted at Frost's capture and led the demand for a treason trial, along with the Monmouth Boroughs' MP Reginald Blewitt. Some witnesses claimed they

The road to Monmouth c. 1840.

Monnow Gatehouse was occupied by the military to prevent any attempt by fellow Chartists to rescue the prisoners, but as the Beacon reported, 'Wednesday and the rest of the week was comparatively tranquil. The excitement had in a great measure passed away, it was now clear that no further danger was to be apprehended'.

Following his interrogation at the Westgate Hotel, and fearing attempts might be made to rescue him, Frost was taken at daybreak on Wednesday 6th November to Monmouth as the *Beacon* reported:

'Shortly after ten o'clock, Frost and Waters, in two separate carriages, attended by constables in each, and surrounded by a body of the 12th Lancers, came up Monnow-street, and preceeded to the jail. They were fully committed on a charge of High Treason. ....Frost appeared pale and haggard. He had with him a carpet bag, which was searched by the direction of Major Marriott, one of the visiting magistrates. He asked for a copy of Burn's Justice and also for pen, ink and paper, and was told that the request would be taken into consideration by the magistrates.'

were being intimidated and, as threats to kidnap them circulated, the authorities moved key witnesses from the coalfield to secure locations in Newport. The Rev. James Coles, when chairing the magistrate's panel, was extremely hostile and condescending to the Welsh-speaking prisoners and threatened to arrest one witness, John Hughes, for 'smiling'.

Two hundred and fifty-three people gave testimony to the examining magistrates at Newport. Fifty men were charged with high treason and as many others with lesser charges.

Within days the government agreed to a treason trial and set up a Special Commission, but concerned about the zealous charging of prisoners by Newport's magistrates, the Home Secretary intervened. A total of twenty-nine prisoners were sent to Monmouth Gaol, of whom twenty-one were charged with high treason. The prison was full to capacity and the Chartists had to share, three men to a cell. The authorities did everything possible to keep them separate from Henry Vincent who was already imprisoned there. Frost, Jones and Williams were placed in the gatehouse and were brought to the holding cells beneath the courtroom at the Shire Hall only on those days when they were on trial.

Monmouth Gaol on the hill behind St Mary's Church.

Holding cells Shire Hall.

Monmouth Gaol from Vauxhall Fields

Monmouth in the limelight
– the Special Commission of Grand Jurors

St Mary's, Monmouth

A Grand Jury met at the Shire Hall to decide which of the Chartist prisoners would stand trial for treason. The three Judges had stayed overnight in Ross and were received on the morning of December 10th at the county border by the Lord Lieutenant, the High Sheriff and an armed retinue, who escorted them to Monmouth.

The Special Commission opened at 10am, after which the court adjourned so that the Judges could go to church at St Mary's. Here the Reverend George Irving preached, '*while they promise them liberty, they themselves are the servants of corruption*', a sermon which was immediately published and sold for 1 shilling a copy.

After the service the Grand Jurors were called at 2pm. One hundred and eighty of Monmouthshire's most influential landowners, the great and the good of the County, wanted to serve. Twenty-three were chosen including the ironmasters

Samuel Homfray and Joseph Bailey, Sir Benjamin Hall MP and J.E.W. Rolls of The Hendre near Monmouth. Other Monmouth men on the Grand Jury included Richard Amphlett, who lived on Castle Hill and Captain Charles Harrison Powell who lived at Parade House. It was their responsibility to decide which of the prisoners should be tried for high treason. It didn't take long. At 3pm the following day a True Bill for high treason was found against fourteen men, including Frost, Williams and Jones for being:

'*Arrayed and armed in warlike manner that is to say with Guns Pistols, Pikes, Swords, Daggers and gathered together against our said Lady the Queen wickedly, maliciously and traitorously did levy and make war against our said Lady the Queen within the realm.*'

Still on the run, Jack the Fifer (John Rees) and Dai the Tinker (David Jones) didn't appear in court.

The Welsh language paper *Seren Gomer* reported on the appearance of the accused in Court:

'*Within a few minutes the sound of wheels and horses was heard outside the Court, and after a short delay the prisoners were led to their appointed place. Everything now was as hushed as the grave, and nothing could be heard but the clinking of the chains as the prisoners came up to the bar, and the occasional quiet whisper of "Which one is Frost?"*'

The court then adjourned until 31st December. Preparations for the Trial continued as a company of 120 Rifles arrived in the town to keep order. Keen to play things down the *Monmouthshire Merlin* claimed:

'*the influx of strangers into Monmouth was not as great as the public anticipated. The hotels were not crowded, and many*

St Mary's from
Hereford Road

Chartist leaders who were not imprisoned, including Feargus O'Connor, arrived in Monmouth. O'Connor had raised funds for Frost to be defended by one of the best legal teams of the day. He and other Chartists, including Hugh Williams, the solicitor from Carmarthen, stayed in Monmouth throughout the trial.

parties who calculated on high renumeration for their lodgings, and held out for tempting offers, were disappointed. The minor hosteleries were, however, filled by witnesses, and arrivals from the manufacturing districts, continued through the day. Order and good arrangement were observable in every quarter, and there appeared really as little excitement, as at ordinary Assizes. The military pacing their rounds, and the London police walking about, told the stranger that there was no want of preparation to meet danger if it approached, and repel any aggressions, if such were attempted to be made, upon the due adminstration of justice.'

But the Government were convinced that the Newport Rising had been an organised rebellion against the state and they wanted to prove it. Interest in events in Monmouth intensified; everyone knew that the penalty for treason was hanging and quartering. Monmouth found itself centre stage at a trial of national importance - the last mass treason trial in Britain.

The treason trial

On a bleak winter's day, 31st December 1839, the last mass treason trial to take place in mainland Britain began. Just after 9am a bugle called and the Lancers and infantry assembled and went to the gaol. When the twelve prisoners arrived at the Shire Hall, handcuffed and chained to each other, they were placed in the holding cells. Ten London policemen ensured that only the magistrates, jury and the members of the press, *'for whom a convenient box had been fitted up to the right of the Grand Jury Box'* were allowed in.

The three Judges walked from the Judges' Lodging at St. James' Mews to the Shire Hall, accompanied by policemen and javelin men. This daily procession was led by Mr Stroud Monmouth's Trumpeter of Assize and six other trumpeters. Train-bearers, gentlemen ushers and the metropolitan police made up the entourage inside the courtroom.

A horn sounded at 10 o'clock, the Judges took their seats and the doors were opened to the public. The courtroom was soon full. Admission to the trials was by ticket only, for which there had been great competition. Then, *'Shortly was heard the clanking of chains, and immediately afterwards the prisoners appeared in front of the dock'*. They stood at the bar in silence. John Frost was the first to be tried. Having been led to believe he was a terrible villain many people were surprised when they saw a 'respectable' gentleman.

For the defence stood two lawyers, one reputedly the most learned and the other the most eloquent of the time. For the prosecution stood the Attorney-General and the Solicitor-General. The scene was set for a show trial.

'A Machine... constructed at Monmouth, under the supervision of the magistrates, by means of which the prisoners will be conveyed from the prison van into the Court, without being annoyed by the crowd that may be then assembled.'

The interior of the court room at the Shire Hall.

The Judges' robing room at the Shire Hall.

The Jury - a fair trial?

When it came to swearing in the Jury over 300 names were called. Many were rejected by Frost's defence team who were extremely concerned Frost wouldn't get a fair trial locally. It was a lengthy process. Thomas Swift, a Monmouth barge owner and boat builder, was just one of the jurors rejected. The Chartist press felt that *'to allow the prisoners to be tried by a middle class Monmouthshire jury was to allow them to be murdered'*. Frost's stepson William Foster Geach tried unsuccessfully to get the trial moved out of the county. He knew many jurors would have read press reports declaring the Chartists guilty of high treason. Some of the reports which appeared in the *Monmouthshire Beacon* in November 1839 were wild in the extreme:

'It has been ascertained that the man who made his way in through the window to the room where the Mayor was, and wounded him with his pike, is a deserter of the 29th regiment, who was hired by Mr. Frost for the purpose of assassinating Mr. Phillips. This of course it would be premature to state as an undoubted fact, but we give it as one of the rumours which are afloat.'

William Foster Geach had been a solicitor in Pontypool but, like his stepfather, had fallen foul of Thomas Prothero and Thomas Phillips and had moved to Bristol. Single handedly and without payment he prepared Frost's defence, work which provided Frost's defence team with the means to challenge the jurors and the witnesses at the trial.

The twelve jurymen eventually selected were all from rural Monmouthshire, and as they were property owners they already had the vote. James Hollings, who ran an ironmongers shop in the town, was the only Monmouth man to sit on the Jury.

The Jury - twelve men good and true.

THE JURY

John Daniel, haberdasher from Abergavenny

Edward Reese, miller from Llanmartin

Thomas Davies, butcher from Abergavenny

Edward Smith, coachmaker from Chepstow

Richard Lewis, farmer from Llanfair Discoed

Christopher John, farmer from Redwick

Edward Brittle, farmer from Mitchell Troy

William Williams, farmer from Llangattock

James Hollings, ironmonger from Monmouth

John Richards, baker from Chepstow

Thomas Jones, farmer, from Nash

John Capel Smith, butcher from Chepstow

Who's Who

The Judges:

Lord Chief Justice, Sir Nicholas Tindal had the confidence and trust of the Home Secretary, Lord Normanby, who didn't want Justice Williams running the Trial, fearing his heavy-handed approach would cause more unrest.

Mr Justice John Williams a Judge with a reputation for savage punishment for those who threatened social order. He sent down the 'Tolpuddle Martyrs' in 1834.

Sir James Parke a learned Judge who was a stickler for technicalities.

The prosecution team:

The prosecution case: that thirty local Chartists including Frost, had met at the Coach and Horses in Blackwood and planned a national rising, and the Chartist leaders were guilty of treason.

Sir John Campbell - The Attorney-General was in charge of the prosecution of all the Chartist prisoners. The Government was convinced that the Newport Rising had been an organised rebellion against the State.

Lord Normanby - The Home Secretary persuaded the Attorney-General to hold the Special Commission and to reduce the number of men charged with treason from 50 to 14.

The defence team:

The defence case: The march on Newport was a demonstration of strength to persuade the Newport magistrates to grant a pardon for Henry Vincent and other Chartist prisoners held in Monmouth Gaol.

Sir Frederick Pollock headed the defence council for Frost. One of the leading barristers of the day, Pollock had previously represented Frost in his case of libel against Thomas Prothero in 1822.

Fitzroy Kelly described as one of the most acute and powerful advocates at the bar and the most eloquent barrister in England.

The Jury

| Prosecution Team | Defence Team | The accused Chartists |

Working out who's who is not easy. The judges either side of Tindall and the accused Benfield and Rees are 'best guesses'!

The Jury

'The Interior of Monmouth Court House faithfully represented during the Trials of Frost, Williams and Jones for High Treason 1839-40.'

To fit all the people into this picture the artist has played a game, turning John Frost's face at a peculiar angle to look directly at the viewer. This was common practice at the time, part of a long tradition in painting of producing contrived commemorative pieces.

Mr Fitzroy Kelly

Sir Frederick Pollock

John Lovell

Richard Benfield

John Rees

John Frost

Zephaniah Williams

William Jones

Charles Walters

Jenkin Morgan

The Trial: The Queen v Frost and others

As soon as the trial opened the Judge, Lord Chief Justice Tindal carefully defined Treason for the Jury as 'the act of raising an army with the intention of going to war against the Crown'. Fourteen men were indicted under the medieval statute of 1356 with leading two thousand and more against the Queen - marching in battle array, seizing arms, forcing subjects of the Queen to join them, attacking the Westgate hotel and firing on the magistrates and Queen's troops. Tindal explained that they were also charged under the 1796 Act with forming a conspiracy that was 'intending or imagining to depose the Queen'. They were accused of planning to get possession of Newport and cut off communications by seizing the mails in order to change the law by force.

In seeking to prove the existence of a conspiracy, the prosecution focused on the Chartist meeting held at the Coach and Horses in Blackwood on the Friday before the Rising. But the only prosecution witness who was at this meeting, William Davies, did not appear at the trial. William was the sweetheart of Ellen, one of John Frost's daughters. He had been with Frost at the Coach and Horses and at the start of the march, but then disappeared. He was arrested at his uncle's house in Canterbury and brought back home to be charged with riot and conspiracy. Having told the magistrates all he knew about the 'Newport plot' he disappeared before the trial began.

This meant that the central 'plank' of the prosecution's case became dependent upon hearsay evidence. Government spies, like David Jones who pursued Vincent, disappeared rapidly after November 4th, but not without leaving a network of informers and vulnerable 'Chartists', who might be 'leaned upon' to give Queen's evidence

James Hodge, John Harford and Job Tovey all claimed to know Frost's intentions. Harford had told the magistrates that he was forced to accompany the Chartists, saying Frost had told: '....all the men were to go armed... and when they got to Stow Hill they were to give three cheers which would produce such an effect on the Mayor that he would die in his bed....and it would produce such an effect on the Soldiers that they would throw down their arms and he would take possession of the Town and stop the Mail for Birmingham

'Monday, The Court resumed its sitting at nine o'clock. Mr. Frost was dressed in a plum coloured coat, and looked better than he did on Saturday.'

… if the mail did not arrive, then the attack would commence in Birmingham, and from thence to the North of England and Scotland'.

As the case proceeded the Attorney-General found that the reliability and consistency of much of this testimony was savaged by the

Sir Frederick Pollock - defender of John Frost.

skillful questioning of Pollock and Kelly. Harford's testimony was discredited when Kelly forced him to reveal that he had spent 12 days under arrest in Newport before giving his statement against Frost and gaining release. Sinisterly, the Court was told that Harford's deposition (his answers to the magistrates) could not be found. Equally James Hodge's story was undermined when he admitted that in advance of examination by the magistrates he had discussed his evidence with Frost's arch enemy, Thomas Prothero, who employed him as a coal miner.

In these circumstances, the Attorney-General decided not to call Hodge's neighbour, Job Tovey, in whose home Frost had lodged during his stay in Blackwood and who had eavesdropped on Frost's conversations. Although the Prosecution had collected evidence from 236 individuals, they only dared bring 38 witnesses forward at Frost's trial.

SIR FREDERICK POLLOCK.
WE shall NEXT WEEK PRESENT to the READERS of the MERLIN
A STRIKING LIKENESS
OF
SIR FREDERICK POLLOCK,
THE DEFENDER OF JOHN FROST,
At the late Trial under the Special Commission; accompanied by a BIOGRAPHICAL SKETCH of that DISTINGUISHED ADVOCATE.—The Engraving will be in the first style of the Art, and its dimensions nine inches by seven. Advertisers are requested to send their favours early in the week, as the Publishers of the MERLIN have made arrangements to put the Paper to press considerably before the usual time. Orders given to the Agents of the MERLIN, and to all respectable Booksellers will prevent disappointments.

ERY, of Monmouth, Gentleman.

ury, of Monmouth, Farmer.

Adams, of Portskewitt, Tailor.

ndrews, of Abergavenny, Ironmonger.

Baber, of Abergavenny, Grocer.

aker, of Abergavenny, Cooper.

wcott, of Abergavenny, Victualler.

Buxton, of Caldico

all, of Chep

Barrow, of

aker, of

er Blun

Bladon,

rt, of

Benne

er B

wler

Baker

ton,

JUST PUBLISHED.

A PORTRAIT of ISRAEL FIRMAN, the INFORMER and PROSECUTOR of the NEWPORT RIOTERS, as taken when on his Examination before the County Magistrates

" The attenuated and sapless frame of Israel Firman, when called to be sworn, produced a mingled sensation of wonder and dread in the Court. His unearthly aspect has so excited the fears of the ignorant in his neighbourhood, that he is popularly regarded as a Sorcerer throughout the district in which he resides. Tall, gaunt, and withered, he stands upright, though exceeding ninety years in age! A profusion of long grisaly hair, flung back from his wrinkled and projecting forehead, gives an expression of great wildness to his features: his sunken and hollow cheeks, shelving eye-brows, piercing and jet black eyes, the fire of which ninety winters have not sufficed to quench, conspired to render his apparition in Court, a thing not to be forgotten ; while his deeply sunburnt complexion and indistinct Asiatic pronunciation, strongly favour the opinion that he belongs to the outcast and wandering progeny of Ishmael."—*Monmouthshire Merlin.*

The Trial continues

The Prosecution decided against producing the most colourful of their witnesses - Israel Firman, who was in Monmouth and had greatly impressed the Grand Jury. The *Merlin* reported:

'Tremendous local interest was roused by the presence in court of the 'sorcerer', Israel Firman, a quack doctor and scissors grinder then living in the neighbourhood. He was ninety-one years of age and had served his apprenticeship as an herbalist in Philadelphia, but by the age of forty-four had been pressed into the British navy at Antigua in the Leeward Islands, and since his release had lived in England. His gaunt, cadaverous appearance, together with the mystery of his life, caused a sensation which his evidence tended to increase'.

Arrested for participating in the riot, Firman claimed he had been forced to go to Newport and turning Queen's evidence, he freely named and accused Chartists. By the time the trial was underway, the authorities began to realize that he had implicated people he couldn't possibly have seen and they decided not to call him.

An important witness for the Crown was Barnabas Brough, a brewer at Pontypool. His evidence demonstrated that Frost was the head of the movement. Brough had been captured by the Chartists in the darkness of 4th November. It seems likely he had been sent by the Lord Lieutenant of Monmouthshire, Capel Hanbury Leigh, to warn the Mayors of Cardiff and Newport about the Chartists' activities. Returning home he was stopped by Chartists who were suspicious of his activities. He was taken to Frost, who knew him and Frost ordered his release.

What happened where and when, according to the witnesses
- Sunday PM, 3rd November to Monday AM, 4th November

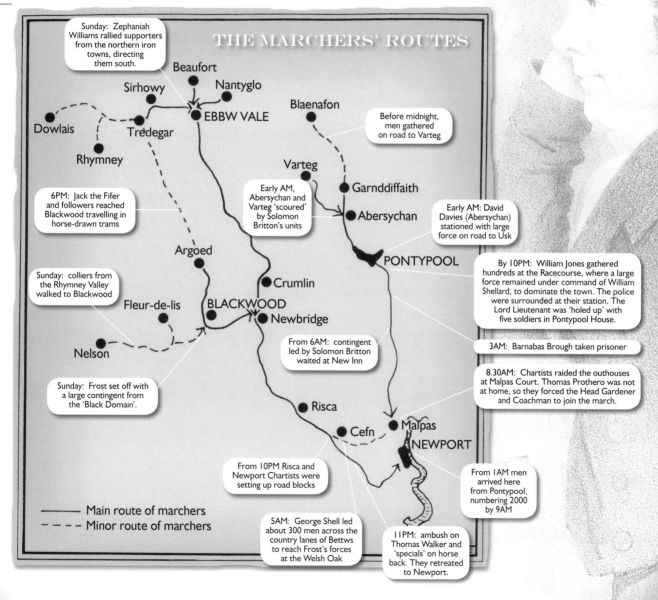

THE MARCHERS' ROUTES

Sunday: Zephaniah Williams rallied supporters from the northern iron towns, directing them south.

Before midnight, men gathered on road to Varteg

Early AM, Abersychan and Varteg 'scoured' by Solomon Britton's units

Early AM: David Davies (Abersychan) stationed with large force on road to Usk

6PM: Jack the Fifer and followers reached Blackwood travelling in horse-drawn trams

Sunday: colliers from the Rhymney Valley walked to Blackwood

By 10PM: William Jones gathered hundreds at the Racecourse, where a large force remained under command of William Shellard, to dominate the town. The police were surrounded at their station. The Lord Lieutenant was 'holed up' with five soldiers in Pontypool House.

3AM: Barnabas Brough taken prisoner

From 6AM: contingent led by Solomon Britton waited at New Inn

8.30AM: Chartists raided the outhouses at Malpas Court. Thomas Prothero was not at home, so they forced the Head Gardener and Coachman to join the march.

Sunday: Frost set off with a large contingent from the 'Black Domain'.

From 10PM Risca and Newport Chartists were setting up road blocks

From 1AM men arrived here from Pontypool, numbering 2000 by 9AM

5AM: George Shell led about 300 men across the country lanes of Bettws to reach Frost's forces at the Welsh Oak

11PM: ambush on Thomas Walker and 'specials' on horse back. They retreated to Newport.

Towns/places: Beaufort, Sirhowy, Nantyglo, Blaenafon, Dowlais, Tredegar, EBBW VALE, Rhymney, Varteg, Garnddiffaith, Abersychan, Argoed, PONTYPOOL, Crumlin, Fleur-de-lis, BLACKWOOD, Newbridge, Nelson, Risca, Cefn, Malpas, NEWPORT

—— Main route of marchers
– – – Minor route of marchers

39

A lengthy speech

Sir Frederick Pollock, in a speech which lasted over five and a half hours, presented the case for the defence. *Seren Gomer* reported how he gave a preliminary overview of all the evidence, showing the weakness of some witnesses and the contradictions of others: '*but however well done his treatment of the matter, we must state that in our opinion he mentioned some matters which did not tend towards the good of the prisoner whom he was defending. He said that he hoped to God that he should not live to see Chartist principles becoming the law of the land, and as he illustrated the five points of the Chartists he said that the equal division of property was among them. Frost said that in this he was mistaken, and that the Chartists had never imagined such a thing*'.

This was a crucial point illustrating how little Chartism was understood by the authorities. Even Frost's defence counsel were unforgivably ill-informed about the People's Charter. The redistribution of property from rich to poor was not a Chartist demand, and never had been!

From a Sketch by Lieut. Taylor, an army draughtsman, showing the direction of army gun fire from the Westgate Hotel. Taylor was despatched to Newport by the authorities to produce a ground plan of the Westgate as part of the official response to what had happened.

Plans and drawings showing what happened at the Westgate mysteriously went missing during the Trial. Local newspapers advertised for their return!

'*The dead figures at the door way are placed as nearly as could be ascertained, when they fell...The plan is not from measurement but sufficiently accurate for explanation: the Pikes denote the points entered by the Chartists: the Firelocks the points defended by the 45th.*'

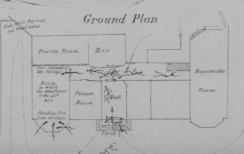

SPECIAL COMMISSION,
MONMOUTH.
THE QUEEN v. FROST AND OTHERS.

WHEREAS various PLANS and DRAWINGS used by the Crown in the course of the above Prosecutions have been TAKEN AWAY by some person or persons from the Crown Court.

Any persons having any such Plans and Drawings are requested to FORWARD THEM FORTHWITH to Mr. T. J. PHILLIPS, or Mr. PHILLS, Solicitors, Newport, to prevent further enquiry.

Guilty?

At the end of Frost's trial Lord Chief Justice Tindal's summing up on January 8th was a sensation. He reminded the Jury of the definition of treason he had given and that they had to establish Frost's intentions. He emphasised that a guilty verdict depended upon 'clear and compatible' evidence from at least two witnesses. Reviewing the prosecution's case Tindal highlighted flaws and inconsistencies in the evidence.

All in the court realised Tindal was summing up for an acquittal, directing the Jury to a verdict of 'not guilty'. The weakness of the case put by the prosecution was clear. Sir John Campbell, the Attorney-General, was convinced the Crown had lost. He need not have worried. The Monmouthshire Jury had already made up their minds. Within 30 minutes they returned to pronounce Frost guilty - with a recommendation to mercy. The Attorney-General had to be recalled from the nearby Beaufort Arms where he had taken his prosecution team for a crisis meeting to sort out what they would do about all the other cases, if Frost was found 'not guilty'.

Chartist fears that the trials would not be fair were justified. Sketches showing three of the Chartist defendants hanging, alongside the words *special fun*, had been drawn by one of the Grand Jurors (J. E. W. Rolls, the grandfather of Charles Rolls of Rolls-Royce fame) on his official papers.

The trials of Zephaniah Williams and William Jones followed in turn and both men pleaded not guilty. But Frost's Jury had set a precedent and guilty verdicts proved inevitable for both of them. Tindal's summing up at John Frost's trial may not have had any effect on the Jury, but it certainly influenced the Attorney-General. Recognising legal flaws in the evidence against the remaining nine men, he speedily engaged in plea bargaining, privately offering reduced sentences in return for admittance of guilt. On January 15th, John Lovell, Charles Waters, Jenkin Morgan, Richard Benfield and John Rees all pleaded guilty before the court.

J.E.W. Roll's doodles of hanging men.

Scribbling by J. E. W. Rolls on his list of prisoners at the Chartist trials in 1839. "Special Fun".

John Frost in court

Their final doom

'The three prisoners Frost, Williams and Jones, were then placed at the bar. They looked pale but composed. If emotion might be said to have been exhibited by any it was by Mr. Frost. He looked paler, and somewhat more emaciated than he did upon his trial. They all looked steadily towards the judges from whom they expected to receive their final doom.' (Merlin 18.1.40)

On January 16th Lord Chief Justice Tindal sentenced those found guilty. The court room was silent as the judges put on their black caps and he pronounced:

John Frost and you, Zephaniah Williams and you, William Jones....be drawn on a hurdle to the place of execution and that each of you be hanged by the neck until you be dead and that afterwards the head of each of you be severed from the body and the body of each be divided into four quarters.

Murmurs of compassion came from the back of the court, but the prisoners remained composed, although Zephaniah Williams apparently had difficulty focussing when the sentence was passed, and listened with his eyes closed. All three were 'taken down'.

The five who had pleaded guilty were now brought to the bar. Tindal proceeded to issue the same death sentence but with recommendation for remission: *'inasmuch as you were not the leaders and contrivers, but rather the ignorant and deluded followers of them, so shall we become humble suitors to Her Majesty that your lives may be spared.'*

Four prisoners who had not pleaded guilty - James Aust, Solomon Briton, George Turner and Edmund Edmonds - were released without punishment. Tindal appreciated that whilst the Whig government needed a 'show trial', it did not want too much 'blood letting'. He had restricted the death penalty to the three middle class ring leaders - Frost, Williams and Jones.

This newsheet, although published in Monmouth, is full or errors and mistakes regarding the Chartists' punishments.

Life inside

Many Chartists had spent Christmas 1839 in Monmouth Gaol, but the *Merlin*'s report of Christmas behind bars gave a false impression of how the Chartists were treated. Zephaniah Williams especially was a shadow of the '*wanted man - 5ft 8 inches, of strong, square build, a bold talker with a blunt manner and a swaggering walk*'. Chained to a gaoler at night he was suffering from sleep deprivation and malnourishment, and having suicidal thoughts. All the prisoners were fed a debilitating diet of potatoes, bread and gruel, which caused many digestive disorders. Frost wrote that his stay at Monmouth Gaol was '*the greatest misery I have endured*', although, in the presence of the Governor, Frost's wife and daughter had been allowed to visit him.

Once the death sentence had been delivered, the editor of the *Merlin* was quick to report the offer of a local surgeon to act as headman, although the paper did back the petition to the Queen calling for clemency, which was organised amongst the inhabitants of Monmouth.

Frost, Williams and Jones shared one room in the gatehouse of the gaol. They could hear the carpenters erecting the gallows on the flat roof above, where executions were held. The *Beacon* reported that John Frost asked for a copy of *Blair's Grave* when the Rev. Mr. Gosling visited the prisoners.

Frost in the condemned cell.

'The debtors and other prisoners in the County Gaol desire to present their best thanks to Joseph Price esq. for their Christmas treat of one pound of beef, one quart of beer, and a quarter-loaf to each prisoner now confined. Mr. Price has long been a benefactor of the imprisoned.'

Monmouth Gaol 1840.

Petitions and a wedding present

There was no right to appeal in 1840 and death sentences were always carried out quickly. The Chartists' legal team had no time to lose and raced to London. During the trial Sir Frederick Pollock had raised objections on procedural technicalities which the Judges agreed should be reviewed by another court. Although unsuccessful in London, his actions delayed the executions for 12 days, time that allowed mass petitions and protest meetings to spread across the country. Two days before the executions were due to go ahead the Prime Minister, concerned about growing public unrest, postponed the date for five days to February 6th.

Sir Frederick Pollock continued to lobby for the Chartists and, as the wedding of Queen Victoria and Prince Albert loomed, so pressure mounted to issue a reprieve. The marriage offered a solution so that no one lost face; it could be seen as a gift of clemency at the time of the Queen's wedding. Pollock was credited with the victory; he had visited Normanby, the Home Secretary, seven times pleading for clemency. But it was Tindal's intervention on 31st January that saved the Chartists. He privately visited the Home Secretary in his Whitehall office and told him that he doubted the evidence brought before the court. Lord Melbourne, the Prime Minister had no choice but to advise the Cabinet that the sentence should be reduced to transportation for life.

Although the *Monmouthshire Beacon* commented, '*We believe there is but one feeling throughout the country as to the commutation of sentence in the case of the Chartist prisoners. All are rejoiced that the unhappy men have escaped the extreme rigour of the law*', this sentiment was not shared by the Monmouthshire magistrates. Reginald Blewitt, Octavius Morgan of the Tredegar Park family and his cousin Samuel Homfray expressed their anger. They wanted heads to roll.

The Prime Minister, Lord Melbourne, who reduced the death sentence to transportation for life. Tindal's role in saving the Chartists' lives was not known until after Queen Victoria's death.

Monmouth attorney J. G. Owen organised a town petition to the Queen for the 'Three Welsh Martyrs', which received wide support.

A spectacle in melancholy

News of the reprieve reached Monmouth Gaol around midnight on 1st February 1840. Frost, Williams and Jones were woken and told of their imminent transportation. At one o'clock, chained and fettered they left the Gaol in a van, guarded by Lancers. One of the few people who saw the prisoners leave described it as, *'peculiarly awful....The wind swept in fitful gusts by the jail-door, and the rain descended in thick drizzling showers'*. No one was allowed to talk to the prisoners, although Frost and Williams spoke to each other in Welsh during the journey to Chepstow. *'They appear to hold themselves aloof from Jones, and eye him with distrust and suspicion, and Jones is taciturn and sullen'*, their guards reported. At Chepstow they boarded a steamer - the 'Usk' - the start of their transportation to Tasmania. As the Press reported, *'The removal of the unhappy men at that hour of the night was a spectacle in melancholy in the extreme.'*

When the 'Usk' called in at St. Ives, there were rumours abroad that local tin miners were planning to rescue them. Throughout the journey they were guarded day and night by two policemen and an armed soldier.

The riverside at Chepstow where Frost, Williams and Jones were placed on the 'Usk' and taken to a prison ship in Portsmouth.

Transportation ...and a knighthood

After a stormy fifteen day journey by sea the prisoners were placed on the *York* prison ship in Portsmouth, before transfer to the *Mandarin* convict ship, where Frost was immediately admitted to the ship's hospital. They were visited by a journalist from the *Beacon* who reported that, '... *they are separate from the other convicts, and they inhabit a cabin of twelve feet in length, and about eight feet in breadth, having three comfortable sleeping berths, a bathing machine, and other conveniences, although dressed in convicts' attire they were not shackled. When visited today at noon Frost was reclining on his berth, and appeared very dejected, but his companions were in good spirits, they had a large supply of books, from which Jones and Williams apparently had been amusing themselves.*'

Other accounts show that they were, in fact, all far from in good spirits, and that Williams was probably suicidal, as well as open to suggestions of mutiny. Frost had been given a letter suggesting that the ship be seized by the convicts and taken to South America. He thought it was probably a trap set for him and dissuaded Williams from taking part. It's likely other pressure was put on the prisoners during the five month voyage. Zephaniah Williams, who had professed his innocence throughout the trial, confessed to the ship's doctor, revealing that the capture of Newport was to have been a signal to Chartists across the country for a general uprising.

As Frost languished on the convict hulk, he wrote to his wife: '*The value of life depends on the use we can be to others; if we cannot use it for the good of family or society it is hardly worth defending.*'

Meanwhile his enemy Thomas Phillips was knighted by the Queen for his brave and defiant stand at the Westgate. *Seren Gomer* reported that Queen Victoria commended him greatly for his wise, determined and unflinching conduct in calming the riot at Newport. He dined with the Queen and the Privy Council, slept at the Palace and in the morning was shown through the splendid rooms, appearing in better health than expected after his recent adventures. His left arm and hand, which were cruelly wounded in the attack on the Westgate, still trouble him badly at times, wrote the correspondent.

Lieutenant Gray was promoted to Captain; the military were honoured with a civic dinner at the Westgate Hotel and were thanked at *'one of the most numerous and respectable assemblies that ever took place in Newport ...held at Williams' great room, Commercial Street. Most of the magistrates and gentry, and all the merchants and respectable tradesmen were present; the mayor presided and thanks were given to the army.'*

Port Arthur penal colony.

Prisoners board a prison ship at Portsmouth.

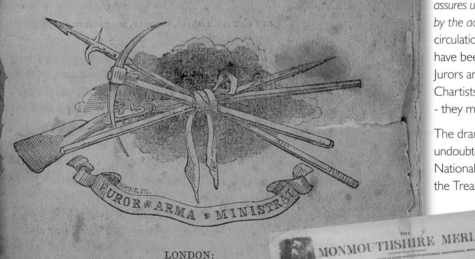

THE

RISE AND FALL

OF

CHARTISM

IN MONMOUTHSHIRE.

"Monte decurrens velut amnis, imbres
Quem super notas aluêre ripas,
Fervet, immensusque ruit——"

HORACE.

LONDON:

A. H. BAILEY & Co., 83, CORNHILL

TO BE HAD OF ALL THE PRINCIPAL BOOKSELLERS IN MONMOUTH
BIRMINGHAM, MANCHESTER, DUBLIN, EDINBURGH, AND T
THE KINGDOM GENERALLY.

1840.

Sensationalising the story

The County had two newspapers. Edward Dowling, a 'Catholic with Whig leanings' edited *The Monmouthshire Merlin*, which was owned by Reginald Blewitt. Generally unsympathetic to the Chartist cause, the *Merlin* was less hysterical in its opposition than its rival the *Monmouthshire Beacon*, which it regularly outsold. The *Merlin* started in Monmouth in 1829 but had moved by 1837 to Newport to gain a greater readership. The *Beacon* was printed in Agincourt Square at Thomas Farror's Works and later in Castle Street. It oozed the establishment view: *'If grievances exist there are constitutional ways of addressing them; but all history assures us that no national good was ever yet achieved by the adoption of physical force.'* With wide circulations across the county, both papers would have been read by the men who stood as Grand Jurors and Jurors. And as both reported that the Chartists were guilty - before they had been tried - they made it impossible for a fair trial to be held.

The drama of the Rising and the showcase trials undoubtedly helped increase newspaper circulation. National interest in the Special Commission and the Treason Trials ensured many journalists arrived in Monmouth to cover the proceedings for the London and provincial press. Special arrangements were made to accommodate them at the Shire Hall, as the local papers reported:

'the approaching Special Commission has rendered necessary the erection of a gallery for the accommodation of Reporters, which has been fixed immediately over the Judge's entrance, and coeval with the Grand Jury box. The press are indebted to the kindness of the visiting magistrates, and to the Mayor of Monmouth, for the provision made for their convenience.'

In an age before photography, no one knew what Frost, Williams or Jones looked like, but everyone wanted to know! Quick to recognise an opportunity Dowling, at the *Merlin*, commissioned pictures of the main protagonists, rushing out a series of pictures:

'*We have just seen a portrait of Mr. John Frost, which gives, with great success, the pensive and calmly resigned expression of features of the convict when hearing the solemn sentence of condemnation pronounced by Chief Justice Tindal. It certainly appears one of the most successful efforts to give correct likeness of this notorious individual, and reflects much credit on the artist, Mr J. F. Mullock.*'

The Chartist Riots were the making of this young artist's career. His lithograph depicting the attack on the Westgate hotel was a 'best seller'. Illustrators were the flavour of the time: within a year of the Monmouth show trial the *Illustrated London News* had been launched as technical developments in lithographic printing revolutionised the publishing world.

As soon as the Trials finished on 16th January printed portraits of the Chartist leaders appeared in the press and were for sale in the streets. The *Beacon* rushed out a 200 page '*Full and correct report of the trial of John Frost for High Treason*', costing one shilling, whilst Dowling at the *Merlin* published a souvenir guide - *The Rise and Fall of Chartism in Monmouthshire*.

The Welsh language press, including papers like *Seren Gomer*, followed events in Monmouth with great interest, whilst the Newport Rising had made world headlines, '*creating an 'extraordinary sensation in France*', as the *Merlin* reported in early December 1839: '*A gentleman just returned to this country from Paris, states that when the exaggerated reports in the newspapers (some of which stated that Newport was in the hands of the Chartists, who were 40,000 strong) first reached the Cafes and Salons, loud and repeated cheers of "Vivent les braves Anglais!" "Vive la Charte Britannique!" resounded through the rooms.*'

The Chartist Rising brought tragedy to Frost's family and many other families across Monmouthshire. His 17 year old son, Henry Hunt Frost, was arrested, taken into custody without a warrant, and brought before the magistrates on November 14th, 1839. Although discharged, he was on the run for many months, the newspapers claiming he had absconded. Henry Hunt died in 1842 at Stapleton, where Frost's wife Mary had moved early in 1840 with her daughters Catherine, Ellen and Anne. Anne was only 13 when her father was sentenced to death and she remained at this Bristol house until after the death of her father in 1877.

William Davies, the sweetheart of Frost's daughter Ellen, was also on the run, having absconded, probably to avoid appearing as a witness (against his girlfriend's father) at Frost's Trial. Staying away for over a year, he later married Ellen.

Frost's stepson William Foster Geach had been a solicitor in Pontypool, until he too had fallen foul of Thomas Prothero and Thomas Phillips in 1837. After the march he represented John Frost, Henry Hunt and others at the Magistrates' examinations, where he crossed swords with

Mr Hallen, who owned the Westgate Hotel in Newport, found that the Chartist Rising was good for business. He claimed £90 for damage to the hotel, and £105 for the special constable's refreshments during the night of the rising!

St Woolos. On Flowering or Palm Sunday, the graves of the Chartists who died at the Westgate were marked with flowers and laurels.

Prothero, who was leading the inquisition. Geach was also Pollock's right hand man at Monmouth throughout the Special Commission. Prothero got his revenge in July 1840. He committed Geach to the Monmouth Assizes where he was sentenced to transportation for gaining false credit.

John Frost's brother, Edward, was arrested and threatened with treason charges, but released when no evidence was produced. A family friend and neighbour, John Partridge, the printer who sheltered John Frost on the night following the Rising, was charged with treason, detained and sentenced at Monmouth to 6 months hard labour for riot and conspiracy. He died, a broken man, in 1844.

Those Chartists who had turned Queen's evidence also found life had changed, and not for the better, as *Seren Gomer* reported:

'We have also heard that there is so much enmity against the witnesses who gave evidence against the Newport Rioters in the industrial workplaces of Monmouthshire that they have had to leave the area, despite the justices' attempts to shelter them and ensure their safety.'

Israel Firman couldn't return home to Blackwood after the Trial. The magistrates paid for him and his family to travel to London by ship. Barnabas Brough went bankrupt; a few months after the Trial his brewery was advertised for sale in the *Monmouthshire Merlin*. An obituary, when his wife died, explained why: '...*in consequence of (being one of the chief witnesses for the Crown at the trial), Mr. Brough became exceedingly unpopular among the colliers who had been concerned in the outbreak, so much so that they deserted the inns he supplied with beer. His once prosperous business soon declined and he was obliged to leave the town'*.

Foreign fortunes

In Tasmania Frost, Williams and Jones experienced extreme hardship and trauma in the Port Arthur penal colony, despite being given the privileges of political prisoners and allowed to keep their own clothes. Instead of being put on heavy road work Frost worked as a clerk in the commandant's office, but a disparaging remark he made about the Colonial Secretary, Lord John Russell, ensured two years' hard labour for him. Later he worked as a school teacher until his pardon in 1854. Still prevented from returning to the UK he toured the USA with his daughter Catherine until 1856, when he was given an unconditional pardon.

Zephaniah Williams worked as a superintendent in the coal mines. As a free man after 1854 he persuaded 100 Welsh miners and their families to join him in Tasmania where he had purchased several coal mines. His wife joined him in 1854 with their daughter Rhoda, but his son Llewelyn only stayed for a few years. Welsh daffodils still flower in the garden of the house Williams built in Tasmania, where he died in 1874.

William Jones worked as an overseer blacksmith in a boys' prison before gaining his freedom. He died in Tasmania, a poor man, in 1783.

Frost was the only one to return to Britain in 1856. Receiving a hero's welcome he lived in Bristol until his death in 1877. By then two of the Charter points had been achieved: the requirement for MPs to own land had been abolished, and the secret ballot box had been introduced. And in 1867 the vote had been granted to all male householders living in towns.

*Port Arthur
then and today.*

Modern democracy starts here

Despite the severity of the punishments dealt to the Monmouthshire Chartists the movement did not die out after 1840. With most of their leaders in prison, by May 1841 the Chartists still managed to collect 1.3 million signatures calling for the pardon of Frost, Williams and Jones. The petition came within one vote of being accepted - the casting vote of the Speaker in Parliament crushed it.

Two further mass Chartist petitions of Parliament were made in 1842 and 1848 (unsuccessfully). In Newport a branch of the National Charter Association (NCA) continued to meet regularly at the Queen Adelaide pub in Griffin Street, although the centre of Chartism in Wales moved west after the Rising, with strongholds in the Glamorganshire Valleys and Merthyr Tydfil surviving well into the 1860s. Merthyr Tydfil with 10 Chartist lodges was one of the most important of the NCA branches, collecting 21,934 signatures for the 1842 National Petition, the fifth largest number for any town in Britain and casting the largest number of votes in the organisation's ballots throughout the 1840s. Its secretary, Morgan Williams was elected to the National Committee. Later, Merthyr Chartist William Gould patented the first secret ballot box.

In 1845 Feargus O'Connor set up the National Land Company. Settling ordinary workers on smallholdings entitled them to the vote, by making them property holders, so the Chartists began buying land and building Chartist cottages. Many of those involved who had taken part in the Rising at Newport

A trade union of agricultural labourers sign a petition for equal electoral reform in the country as well as the towns.

Snig End Chartist cottages in Worcestershire, built by the National Land Company.

Chartism and you...

continued to support Chartist ideas, even those who had served prison sentences. John Lovell and Charles Waters, after their release from Mill Bank Prison, became supporters of the Chartist Land Company and played a role in the revival of Chartism in 1847 - 48.

Although Chartism continued as a radical force pushing for political reform, it became much more than a movement to secure constitutional change. It was the power behind the great social legislation of the 19th century. Chartist activities gave ordinary men and women the confidence to pursue these agendas, launching them into trade unionism, miners institutes, working men's libraries, cooperatives and the political movements of Liberalism, Labour and women's suffrage.

... we're all involved in this story

What happened in Newport and Monmouth led to the establishment of democracy in Britain and in many other countries around the world. Most of the Chartists' demands, except for annual parliaments, have now been realised. They are the foundation of our modern democracy and they affect us every day. We can vote in General Elections and, if we choose, stand for Parliament - because Chartists were prepared to die for what they believed in. Chartism was the world's first independent working-class political movement - and the first great show of popular protest in Britain's history.

Chartists demonstrating in London in 1848.

And finally...

John Frost in old age.

What was all the fuss about? Was the Newport Rising a revolution, or a riot?

Were the events at Newport in 1839 intentionally 'revolutionary'? Was it an attempt to overthrow the political system or just a protest demonstration that got out of control?

The authorities believed they had stopped a rebellion. The frightened landed and commercial classes were convinced that had it not been for Gray and his soldiers they would have been killed in their beds. They could not understand why a successful businessman like Frost, who had once been the mayor and a magistrate, had betrayed them.

From Birmingham to Newcastle, Chartists had been expecting news from Newport. Magistrates in the West Country were convinced that they would be next to see trouble. London supporters were observed waiting apprehensively. Last minute attempts were made to restrain the headstrong militants of Monmouthshire and a mysterious messenger from Bradford visited Frost in Blackwood.

A mass rising had been discussed by the People's Convention but no plans had been laid. The south Wales lodges followed their own path - they wanted to release their hero Vincent from Monmouth Gaol, but Frost directed them to advance to Newport. Frost's defence team maintained he led the protest to Newport to demand support for clemency from the magistrates who had charged Vincent and the three Newport Chartists with sedition.

There is no doubt that Frost targeted the civil authorities. He carefully avoided contact with the soldiers at the Workhouse and marched towards the Mayor's headquarters at the Westgate. When the crowd arrived at the hotel, they could not see any soldiers and they attempted to occupy the building, protected by the hated special constables.

Did Frost naively expect his heavily armed forces to voice their complaints and go home without violence? Did he assume that Newport was a Chartist town because the cause had won immense support there? Perhaps he hoped that the authorities, faced by overwhelming numbers, would play for time and be conciliatory. In demanding that the Magistrates give way to the people's will, he was challenging the authority of the state. What if the authorities melted away? He must have appreciated that this would create a revolutionary situation. His faith in the power and right of the people to resist tyranny meant that he was encouraging his followers to seize power locally. The results of such success would be momentous.

And what would they do if the magistrates resisted? Disingenuously both Zephaniah Williams and Frost reminded their followers that their weapons were carried only in self-defence and urged them to 'keep the peace'. They encouraged the belief that the soldiers would not fire. As Frost led his forces into Newport, he must have been not only surprised by the strength of the forces ranged against him in the town, but also troubled by the sinister elements positioned within his own ranks. For months underground 'cells' had been arming and drilling in the coalfield and the money collected by the lodges, used to purchase guns and pay for the manufacture of pikes.

As the years passed, the Chartists maintained that the violence at Newport had been the act of hired traitors - an understandable reaction in the 1840s when the movement endured the full vengeance of the State - mass imprisonments, many transportations and no clemency for the three 'Welsh Martyrs'. Feargus O'Connor was convinced that a deserter from the 29th Regiment had been an *'agent provocateur'*.

Frost wrote nothing and rarely said anything about the Rising, but once during a public lecture he declared that Hodge and Harford, two Prosecution witnesses, *'must have been government agents, for I have never spoken to them in my life, and the story of the Welsh mail which they gave in evidence was nothing but a foul and flagitious falsehood'*.

William Jones, protesting his innocence in 1840 claimed: *'Persons employed by them as spies knew well our intentions were not treasonable, that the attack on the Westgate was never contemplated, and was only put in practice by the Emiseries of the magistrates, some of whom unfortunately fell a sacrifice to their perfidy'*.

What do you think?

Chartist ancestors

It was not unusual for enthusiastic Chartists to name their children after the Chartist leaders. John Frost, Henry Vincent and William Lovett were popular names in the 1840s. Some children were even given the name Charter or Charters. If you come across one of these names in your family tree, it is highly likely you have Chartist ancestors!

Some Chartists did all they could to distance themselves from the events of 1839, trying to erase the episode from family memory. Sylvia Taylor who grew up in Newport in the 1940s remembers her grandmother talking about a Chartist in the family. Soldiers had come looking for him, but he had escaped by hiding up a chimney. Sylvia discovered that he was eventually convicted of conspiracy, sedition and riot, but not until October 1840, when he was captured and tried in Usk. His three years' hard labour at Monmouth Gaol included time on the treadmill. This part of the story the family had chosen to forget. Her ancestor was *Wright Beatty*, and by pleading guilty he avoided seven years' transportation. On his release from gaol in 1843 he was probably blacklisted by local employers and had to move away to find work. There is no trace of where or when he died.

Sylvia Taylor shared her Chartist ancestor discovery with readers of Who do you think you are? magazine.

Tracing their Chartist ancestors - Sylvia Taylor, Patricia Horner, Rita Catton, Valerie Gordon, Bill O'Kee and others in the dock at the Shire

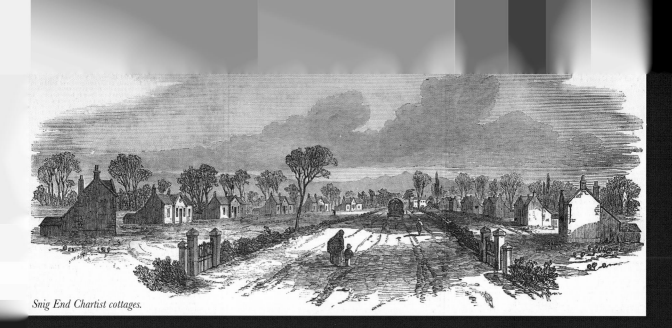

Snig End Chartist cottages.

Newport's Chartist mosaic.

Valerie Gordon and her sister Rita Catton discovered that John Jarrett Lovell, one of the 14 Chartists charged with high treason, was their great-great-great uncle. Lovell was seriously wounded at the Westgate and taken into custody at the Stow Hill Workhouse, where he spent 33 days recovering. At his trial he pleaded guilty and was sentenced to death, but his punishment was commuted through plea bargaining to imprisonment with hard labour at Mill Bank. Prison did little to change his views, and after his release in 1844 he returned to Newport and his wife, and in 1847 is recorded as a subscriber to the Chartist Land Company. He died in 1852.

Millions of people signed the three petitions presented to Parliament in 1839, 1842 and 1848 - one of them may have been your ancestor. Sadly these documents have been destroyed, but lists of the special constables and those in the military survive. You might find ancestors who were on the establishment side or fought in the military like Lieutenant Gray!

Milestones to Modern Democracy

12th July 1839	1st Charter petition presented to Parliament and rejected.
4th Nov 1839	Chartist march to Newport and attack on the Westgate
6th Nov 1839	John Frost arrives at Monmouth Gaol
8th Nov 1839	Dead chartists buried at St Woolos Church, Newport
31st Dec 1839	Chartist trials begin in Monmouth
16th Jan 1840	Chartist leaders found guilty, and sentenced to death
1st Feb 1840	Chartist sentences reduced to transportation for life
2nd Feb 1840	Frost, Williams and Jones taken to Chepstow to board the steamer *Usk*
30th June 1840	Frost, Williams and Jones arrive at Port Arthur penal colony, Tasmania
May 1842	2nd Chartist Petition to Parliament with 3.3m signatures
April 1848	3rd Chartist petition to Parliament
July 1854	Frost receives news of his conditional pardon

Understanding the Jargon

Agent Provocateur - an undercover agent, employed to gain the trust of suspects to tempt them to do something illegal so they can be arrested and punished.

Assizes - judicial courts held in England and Wales up to 1971, replaced by Crown Courts.

Attorney - a lawyer or somebody legally empowered to make decisions and act on someone else's behalf.

Attorney-General - the government's chief legal officer and adviser.

Commutation - the reduction of a sentence to a less severe punishment.

Constituency - a single area, defined by boundaries, for the purpose of electing an MP.

Democracy - a type of government in which power is invested in the people as a whole, exercised on their behalf by elected representatives.

Grand Jury - a panel of 23 jurors who decide if there are grounds for a trial.

Indictment - a formal accusation and written accusation of a serious crime presented to court.

Libel - false and malicious written statements that damage someone's reputation.

Nonconformist - member of a church or chapel outside the established Church of England.

All political prisoners pardoned

Property qualification for MPs abolished

Secret voting introduced

3rd Reform Act - 2 out of 3 men now eligible to vote

All men and women over 21 can vote

May 1856

12 July 1856

1858

1867

1872

27 July 1877

1884

1918

1928

1948

1969

Frost returns to Britain

2nd Reform Act gives many working class men living in towns the vote

Frost dies in Bristol

All men over 21 and women over 30 gain the right to vote

Independent Electoral Commission established to create constituencies

Everyone over 18 has the right to vote

Pew Rent - money paid to secure seats in a particular pew in church.

Queen's Evidence - evidence for the prosecution, given by someone who took part in the crime, in exchange for leniency.

Riot Act - English law (1714-1973) which said people making a public disturbance had to disperse within an hour of the act being read to them by a magistrate.

Sedition - words or actions designed to incite or provoke rebellion against the government.

Special Commission - when faced with serious offences threatening order, such as treason and sedition, the Government had authority to appoint a Special Commission to hear a case quickly.

The Black Domain - the Monmouthshire coalfield between Nelson and Crumlin, where 'sale' coal was produced.

The People's Charter - six constitutional reforms of Parliament demanded by the Chartists.

Tory - Aristocratic supporters of the Stuart King after the restoration. During Victoria's reign they became the Conservative Party.

Transportation - exile to Tasmania, as punishment.

True Bill - approval for a trial of somebody to take place.

Whig - Aristocrats who feared the return of the Stuarts. They were supporters of the Glorious Revolution of William and Mary in 1688. In Victoria's reign they became the core of the Liberal Party.

Monmouth's Chartist places

A short walk around Monmouth will take you to many locations associated with the Chartist trials.

We've numbered the sites on an old map so you can see what Monmouth was like in 1836. Priory Street was constructed soon afterwards; you can see the dotted line of the proposed new road. Several buildings were demolished to allow access to Agincourt Square.

1. The Shire Hall - scene of the trials in 1839-1840

2. The Beaufort Arms Hotel. Many visitors to the town during the trial would have stayed here.

3. The *Monmouthshire Beacon* was printed on Castle Hill. Here, straight after the trial, the public could obtain for 1 shilling *A History of the Rise and Fall of Chartism in Monmouthshire*. Richard Amphlett, one of the Grand Jurors also lived on Castle Hill.

4. The White Swan Hotel, White Swan Court, where the 12th Lancers were billeted during the trials.

5. The Nelson Museum and Local History Centre on Priory Street has a Chartist archive.

6. St. Mary's. The Judges attended church here immediately before the trials began.

7. Monmouth solicitor Mr J. G. H. Owen lived in Monk Street. He organised Monmouth's petition to save the Chartists from execution.

8. Parade House, home of Captain Charles Harrison Powell who sat on the Grand Jury.

9. Site of Monmouth Gaol, where Frost, Vincent and other Chartists were imprisoned in the gatehouse, which is the only part surviving today.

10. Monmouth Cemetery where you can find the grave of Mr Stroud the trumpeter.

11. The Judges' Lodging in St. James' Mews, where the Judges stayed during the trial. Police protection is nothing new: St. James' Mews were guarded day and night throughout the trial.

12. Almshouse Street. Mr R. Stroud, the trumpeter who looked after the prisoners in the holding cells at the Shire Hall, lived here on his retirement.

13. The Bell Assembly Rooms (now the Savoy Theatre). Henry Vincent spoke at a Chartist meeting here in March 1839. The meeting attracted many Monmouth radicals despite the town being very 'Toryfied and under the influence of the Duke of Beaufort'.

14. The town's only Jury member, James Hollings, ran an ironmonger shop in Monnow Street.

15. The Rope Works where Chartist sympathiser John Cloud worked. He was a supporter of O'Connor's Land Plan.

16. The Masons Arms. This pub had a colourful reputation. Before the trials the landlord, William Pritchard, was ordered to appear before the Mayor of Monmouth, and threatened with penalties if he sold beer to anyone who called themselves a Chartist!

17. Monnow Gate, through which the Chartist prisoners would have entered the town.

With thanks to David Harrison.
Why not pick up his Monmouth Chartist Trail leaflet?

Proud of our Chartist past

The Chartist trail spreads right across south Wales. Here are some nearby Chartist places you might like to explore.

1 Pay your respects to the men who died at the Westgate Hotel by visiting St. Woolos Cathedral in Newport. Every year on 4th November people gather at St. Woolos graveyard to remember the men who died on this date in 1839.

2 At Newport Museum and Library in John Frost Square see pistols carried by Chartists on the march to Newport, as well as other Chartist memorabilia.

3 Visit the Chartist Centre at Salem Chapel in Blaina to find out about Chartism in Blaenau Gwent.

4 If you think you have Chartist ancestors you can find official documents at Gwent Archives which has a large collection of original documents about the Chartists.

5 Follow the Chartist Trail around the Eastern Valley from Pontypool, the home of William Jones, George Shell and Capel Hanbury Leigh, to Blaenavon. http://trails.visittorfaen.co.uk/trails/chartism.aspx

6 Immerse yourself in the Chartist period. Pick up a copy of Alexander Cordell's *Rape of the Fair Country* and follow the Cordell Country Tour to sites such as the grave of Sir Thomas Phillips in Llanelen churchyard, near Abergavenny.

7 The town of Blackwood's association with Chartism is remembered in the new Chartist bridge.

8 After the Rising Merthyr Tydfil had one of the largest Chartist Lodges in the UK and continued to campaign for the vote long after the 1839. A Merthyr Chartist, William Gould patented the secret ballot box. A Chartist Trail around the town highlights Chartist pubs and the church where a peaceful sit-in was held in August 1839.

9 Enjoy a stroll along the riverside in Chepstow, but spare a thought for how Frost, Williams and Jones must have felt as they boarded the steamer *Usk* here in February 1840.

10 Monmouth where the Chartists were imprisoned in the County Gaol and tried at the Shire Hall.

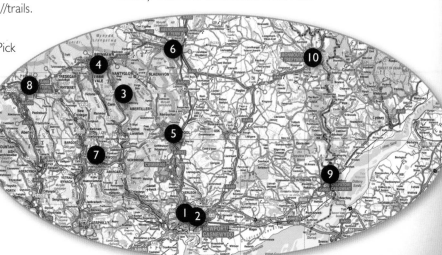

Contains Ordnance Survey data © Crown copyright and database right 2011

Where the pictures come from

Allport Library and Museum of Fine Arts, Tasmanian Archive and Heritage Office
Etablissement Penitentiare de Port Arthur (p.47), Port Arthur (p.51)

Blorenge Books
Rape of the Fair Country (p.62)

Chepstow Museum
Riverside at Chepstow (p.45)

Getty Images
Charter Cartoon (p.5, p.55), Feargus O'Connor (p.8, 31), General Chartist Convention 1839 (p.11), Customers in a pub c. 1825 (p.12), Detail from engraving - Birmingham union meeting, 1832 (p.13), Chartists occupy church (p.15) Giant Chartist Petition (p.18, 53, 56),Daniel O'Connell (p.27) Wedding of Queen Victoria and Prince Albert (p.44), Queen Victoria (p.46), Convict ship at Portsmouth (p.47), Agricultural labourers' union (p.52), Chartist Petition 1848 (p.53)

National Portrait Gallery
William Lovett (p.4 & 8), John Frost (p.5), Lord Chief Justice Sir Nicholas Tindal (p.34), Sir John Campbell (p.34), Lord Normanby (p.34, 44), Lord Melbourne (p.44)

Nelson Museum & Local History Centre
Monmouth Shire Hall (p.2), Gate on Monmouth Bridge (p.3 , 29, 61), View of Monmouth 1844 (p.3, 28), Monmouth Market (p.3, 61) Extracts from The Monmouthshire Merlin and Monmouthshire Beacon November 1839 - March 1840 (p.14, 19, 24, 37, 38, 40, 48, 49, 50),Monmouth Gaol, Waugh (p.29), Monmouth (p.29),Monmouth from the Hereford Road (p.30), St Mary's Church (p.31), Monmouth from the Kymin (p.31), Israel Firmin in The Monmouthshire Merlin (p.38), Rolls doodles of prisoners hanging (p.41), St Woolos from Hall's South Wales, the Wye and the Coast (p.50), 1836 map of Monmouth (p.61), Shire Hall - plan of 1724 (back cover)

Newport Museum & Heritage Service
The Attack on the Westgate (front cover), 'The Welch Chartist Martyrs' (inside cover, p.44), Mr. John Frost 'Condemned to DEATH for high treason' (p.6), 'Chartist Chief No.3 Jones of Pont-y-pool on his trial taking notes of a Witness Deposition' (p.7), Detail from the Attack on the Westgate (p.8 & 22), Thomas Prothero (p.8 & 27), Thomas Phillips (p.8, 46), Chartist Newspaper and Broadsheet (all p.8, 16), St Woolos (p.14), The King's Head Hotel, Newport (p.16), Newport 1836 (p.23), The Chartist attack at Newport, 1839 (p.24), Attack on the Westgate (p.25), Detail from Attack on the Westgate (p.26), The Westgate from Rise & Fall of Chartism 1840 (p.27), Detail from The Rise and Fall of Chartism 1840 (p.32, 43, 48), Sir John Campbell (p. 34), Sir Frederick Pollock in The Rise and Fall of Chartism (p.34, 37, 38, 40), The Interior of Monmouth Courthouse faithfully represented during the trials of Frost Williams and Jones for high treason 1839-40 (p.33, 34, 35), John Frost at his Trial (p.36), 'Chartist Chief' No.2 Zephaniah Williams as he appeared on his Trial January 10th 1840 (p.39), Picture and Ground Plan of the Westgate Hotel (p.40), 'Chartist Chief' No. 1 John Frost as he appeared on his Trial January 10th 1840 (p.41), Three Chartists, from Rise and Fall of Chartism 1840 (p.42), Sentence of the Prisoners (p.42), Photograph of John Frost (p.54), Attack on the Westgate (p.56)

Port Arthur Historic Site Management Authority (p.51)

Rhondda Cynon Taff Digital Archive
Dr William Price (p.7)

Barrie Trinder
Henry Vincent (p.6 & 17)

Sherwood Foresters Regimental Museum
45th Foot Regiment (p.9, 21)

Llanidloes Museum
Wanted poster (p.28)

Pat Drewett
Newport Mosaic (p.56-7, 62)

Private collection
Chartist Cottages at Snig End (p.52, 56)

All other images from the Shire Hall collections

Further reading

Malcolm Chase *Chartism: a New History* (2007)

Edward Dowling *The Rise and Fall of Chartism in Monmouthshire* (1840)

Peter J. R. Goodall *Down through the trap door. The history of Monmouth and Usk Gaols* (2010)

J. Gurney and T. Gurney *Transcript of the Trial of John Frost for High Treason* (1840)

David J. Harrison *Monmouth and the Chartists* (2004)

David J. Harrison *Monmouth Town Chartist Trail* (2009)

John Humphries *The man from the Alamo* (2004)

W.N.Johns *The Chartist riots at Newport, November 1839* (Fiftieth Anniversary 1889)

David J.V. Jones *The last rising: the Newport insurrection of 1839* (1985)

Micheal Miller *The British Army and Internal Security 1815-1850*

David Osmond 'After the Rising: Chartism in Newport 1840-48', *Gwent Local History* number 98, Spring 2005

Stephen Roberts and Dorothy Thompson *Images of Chartism* (1998)

Eric Wiles *Chepstow and the Chartists* The Chepstow Society

Ivor Wilks 'Insurrection in Texas: the Careers of John Rees' *Welsh History Review* volume 11 1982-83

Ivor Wilks *South Wales and the rising of 1839* (1984)

David Williams *John Frost: a study in Chartism* (1939)

Norman Wybron *Chartists of Blaenau Gwent* (1989)

Trial Papers held at Newport Reference Library, John Frost Square, Newport

Copies of *Seren Gomer*, *The Monmouthshire Merlin* and *The Monmouthshire Beacon* between 1838 and 1841

http://chartists.net/ - the Chartist Ancestors website

Thank you

Thank you to the following for advice and encouragement and for allowing images to be reproduced in this book.

Kim Colebrook, Pat Drewett, Lindsay Fowke, Ian Parkin, Karin Molson, Mike Booth, David Harrison, Colin Gibson, Andrew Helme, Barrie Trinder, Annie Rainsbury, Jenny Lewis and Andrea Endreweit.

Chepstow Museum
Getty Images
Gwent Archives
Llanidloes Museum of Local History and Industry
National Portrait Gallery
Nelson Museum and Local History Centre, Monmouth
Newport Reference Library
Newport Museum and Art Gallery
Port Arthur Historic Site Management Authority
Rhondda Cynon Taff Digital Archive
Sherwood Foresters Regimental Museum
Tasmanian Archive and Heritage Service

This book has been produced as part of the restoration programme of the Shire Hall which has been funded by the Heritage Lottery Fund. This elegant building would not have been returned to its former glory without the energy, determination and enthusiasm of the Shire Hall stewards and the local community. This book is dedicated to everyone who played a part in the restoration of the Shire Hall.

Editorial team: Ruth Waycott, Les James, Elin ap Hwyel.

Ruth Waycott is a freelance writer and interpreter, based in Monmouthshire. Les James, is Research Associate, at the South Wales Centre for Historical and Interdisciplinary Research, University of Wales, Newport. Elin ap Hwyel is a freelance writer and interpreter, working in English and Welsh, based near Aberystwyth.

Design by Olwen Fowler.
Print by Cambrian Printers.

Published by the Shire Hall, Monmouth
www.shirehallmonmouth.org.uk
Copyright Monmouthshire County Council 2011
ISBN 978-0-9568745-0-4

monmouthshire
sir fynwy

Supported by
The National Lottery
through the Heritage Lottery Fund

cefnogwyd gan
y loteri genedlaethol
trwy gronfa dreftadaeth y loteri